The Old Norse Poetic Translations of Thomas Percy

MAKING THE MIDDLE AGES

4

MAKING THE MIDDLE AGES
VOLUME 4

THE CENTRE FOR MEDIEVAL STUDIES
UNIVERSITY OF SYDNEY, AUSTRALIA

The Old Norse Poetic Translations of Thomas Percy

A New Edition and Commentary

Margaret Clunies Ross

BREPOLS

British Library Cataloguing in Publication Data

Percy, Thomas, 1729-1811
    The Old Norse poetic translations of Thomas Percy : a new edition and
    commentary. – New ed. – (Making the Middle Ages ; 4)
    1.Old Norse poetry – Translations into English
    I.Title II.Clunies Ross, Margaret
    839.6'1

    ISBN 2503510779

© 2001, Brepols Publishers n.v., Turnhout, Belgium

D/2001/0095/127
ISBN 2-503-51077-9

Printed in the E.U. on acid-free paper.

Contents

Acknowledgements

My principal acknowledgement in the preparation of this book is to the Rare Books and Special Collections Library of Fisher Library, University of Sydney, for permission to use their copy of Thomas Percy's *Five Pieces of Runic Poetry* (1763) as the basis of this facsimile edition. Thanks are due in particular to Ms Kate Sexton, Associate Librarian, Reader Services, and Mr. Neil Boness, Rare Book and Special Collections Librarian, for giving permission for a scan to be made of the book and for it to be used in preparing the facsimile edition. I am particularly grateful to Fisher Library for waiving reproduction fees that would normally apply for this purpose. I also thank Ms Smadar Gabrieli for carrying out the scan.

My research into Thomas Percy's work in Old Norse studies has been greatly assisted by librarians at several relevant libraries that have significant Percy collections. I have greatly benefitted from being able to inspect what remains of Percy's own library in the Special Collections section of The Queen's University Library, Belfast, and I am particularly indebted to Mr. Michael Smallman and Miss Mary Kelly for their assistance to me while I was in Belfast and in answering various queries sent from Sydney. As always, staff in Duke Humfrey's Library at the Bodleian Library, Oxford, and in the Manuscripts and Rare Books Libraries at the British Library provided a high level of professional service that is of great assistance to a researcher in this field, especially to one making short visits from Australia.

Finally, I am indebted to Mr. Simon French for the great care he has taken in formatting and preparing my manuscript for publication.

Abbreviations and Short Titles

BL: British Library

Finnur Jónsson A I and B I: Jónsson, Finnur ed. 1912-15, *Den norsk-islandske skjaldedigtning*. A I-II (tekst efter håndskrifterne), B I-II (rettet tekst). Gyldendal, Copenhagen, repr. Rosenkilde & Bagger, Copenhagen, 1967 (A) and 1973 (B).

LP: Finnur Jónsson, *Lexicon Poeticum Antiquæ Linguæ Septentrionalis. Ordbog over det norsk-islandske skjaldesprog oprindelig forfattet af Sveinbjörn Egilsson*. 2nd. edn. Copenhagen: S. L. Møller, 1931. Rpt. 1966.

OED: *The Oxford English Dictionary*, prepared by J. A. Simpson and E. S. C. Weiner, 2nd. edn. 20 vols. Oxford, Oxford University Press, 1989.

A Note on the Translation
of Skaldic Verse

Most of the poetry that Thomas Percy translated from Old Norse belongs to a corpus of medieval Scandinavian verse that modern scholars call skaldic, after the Old Norse word for a poet, *skáld*. There were two kinds of medieval Scandinavian poetry, eddic and skaldic, and, although we cannot draw a hard-and-fast line between them, eddic poetry is a Scandinavian development of the common Germanic alliterative verse-form and generally more straightforward, both in diction and word order, than skaldic verse. The latter seems to have originated at the courts of the kings and earls of Norway in the ninth century, but, although it continued to be composed by Norwegians, particularly in honour of their kings, Icelanders became the most skilful practitioners of this esoteric art both in the latter part of the Viking Age and well into the Christian era. Some Danish and Swedish kings and their entourages seem to have appreciated skaldic verse, which was probably also practised at the Anglo-Saxon courts of Danish rulers before the Norman Conquest. Skaldic poetry began as a court poetry, and its chief objective was to praise and record the deeds of the aristocrats and rulers who patronised its poets. However, in Iceland its role extended to commemorate people who were not aristocrats as well as notable events in individuals' lives.

Skaldic verse was a kind of literature intended for the intellectual elite of a society that put a very high value on the art of poetry. During the Viking Age it was an oral art which entered the written record embedded for the most part in long prose narratives, or sagas, of the thirteenth and fourteenth centuries but it also survived the transition from orality to literacy and paganism to Christianity independently, so that many skalds from the twelfth century onwards were both Christian and literate. The diction of skaldic poetry is complex and difficult and its word order often fractured and unlike that of prose. In respect of its diction skaldic poetry resembles the riddle, in respect of its fractured syntax, the crossword puzzle. These characteristics made – and still make – the understanding and translation of skaldic verse into modern languages very difficult. It was particularly difficult for eighteenth-century translators like Thomas Percy, because their understanding of Old Norse, and Norse poetic diction, was quite limited, and they generally translated from editions with Latin paraphrases of the Old Norse texts that were often based on the readings of inferior manuscripts.

One of the greatest problems for any translator of skaldic verse is its kennings, which are periphrastic noun phrases, generally comprising two nouns, one in a genitival relationship to the other, which together refer to a third noun, which is not indicated at all in the poetic text. For example, *Gerðr gollhrings*, 'Gerðr of the gold ring', is a kenning for a woman, not necessarily a specific woman, but an aristocratic woman in her generic role as the wearer of gold ornaments in the form of arm rings. We find this kenning used in the verses of the Norwegian king Haraldr the hard-ruler which Percy translates as 'The Complaint of Harold'. In order to understand this simple kenning, and many of them are much more complex than this, the reader or audience needs to know that Gerðr is the name of a Norse giantess who marries the god Freyr and that, according to the conventions of skaldic verse, her name could be substituted by the generic concept 'woman' when it was accompanied by a determinant such as 'gold ring'. Many concepts that could have been represented by simple nouns in skaldic poetry are represented by kennings instead.

The nature of the skaldic kenning posed several problems for translators such as Percy and presents comparable problems for modern translators. The first problem, which was often insoluble for them, was to understand the meaning of the individual elements of the kenning (often expressed by abstruse poetic vocabulary) and then to understand what the kenning as a whole meant, that is, what its referent was. Even well-informed Icelandic scholars of Percy's day sometimes misunderstood the kenning-system and its referents. The second problem was how to translate the poetry so that the non-specialist reader, who lacked a knowledge of Norse mythology and early Scandinavian culture, could understand what was meant without being overwhelmed with notes. Most editors and translators of the period – and indeed some of the present day – solved this problem by suppressing the two constitutive elements of the kenning (which we call base-word and determinant) and 'translating' only the referent which, as we have seen, does not actually appear in the Norse texts at all. Thus, to take the example I gave above, when translators encountered a phrase like 'Gerðr of the gold ring' they would substitute 'woman' or another simplex with roughly similar meaning. In this process a great deal of the text's meaning and poetic character are lost.

As he explains in the Preface to *Five Pieces of Runic Poetry*, Percy adopted a position of compromise in the task of translating Norse poetry. He realised that he should not burden his readers with what we might call 'information overload', but he also recognised that, in order to impress them with the esoteric and exotic nature of this, to them, new literary experience, he should introduce some judicious examples of what he considered the ancient Scandinavians' wild and barbarous poetic imagination. In my notes to his translation, I frequently analyse how Percy and his sources handled the Old Norse texts, and this requires me to discuss kennings. In order to show the reader the differences between Percy's version and what the medieval texts actually say, I have 'unpacked' the kennings according to a system used by the editors of a new edition of the corpus of Old Norse-Icelandic skaldic poetry, which is in progress. These rules are to be found in Clunies Ross *et al.* 2000, 33-4.

My 'unpacked' kennings, in which the individual meanings of both the two constitutive elements and the referent are revealed, are explained in square brackets immediately after the literal translation of both base-word and determinant. The sense of the referent, that is, the kenning's referential meaning, is given in small capitals. Where the kenning includes the name of a known mythological personage, that name is explained after the proper noun, e.g. Gerðr [giantess]. Where an alternative name for a mythological being is used (which is not the name by which he or she is most commonly known), the 'normal' name is given thus after the name actually used, e.g. Yggr [=Óðinn]. Thus in explaining the kenning *Gerðr gollhrings*, I give the English translation followed by the identification of the kenning referent, viz. 'Gerðr [giantess] of the gold ring [WOMAN]'. Sometimes one or more kennings form the determinants of another, which encloses it. In such cases the innermost kenning, as it were, is given first in the translation, with an arrowhead indicating that it becomes the determinant of the outer kenning or kennings. An example is *skers Haka skíðgarðr*, 'the ski-fence of Haki's [sea-king] skerry [SEA>SHIP>ROW OF SHIELDS], a kenning that we find in 'The Ransome of Egill the Scald'.

Five Pieces of Runic Poetry
Bodley MS Percy c. 7
and the present edition

Thomas Percy published *Five Pieces of Runic Poetry* with R. and J. Dodsley in Pall Mall on 14 April 1763. The slim volume was anonymous. It was nearly two years since he had obtained a signed agreement from James Dodsley, on 21 May 1761, to publish '*five* pieces of *Runic Poetry translated from the Islandic Language*'.[1] Percy acknowledged the delay in publication, somewhat disingenuously, with a note facing the Preface, claiming that 'the publication has been delayed by an accident'.[2]

---

[1] The agreement has been preserved as Oxford, Bodleian Library MS Eng. Lett. d. 59, *Correspondence of Bishop Percy*, f. 8r: 'Whereas Thomas Percy, Clerk, has this day sold me the property of two pamphlets, the one containing *A New Version of Solomon's Song*: the other *five* pieces of *Runic Poetry translated from the Islandic Language*: I hereby engage to pay to the said Thomas Percy \or his Executors/ on Demand ten guineas for each of the said pamphlets\which intitles me to full profits of first impression of each/ on demand: as also ten guineas for every thousand that shall be printed of all future Impressions of each pamphlet separately: and whenever the said pieces shall be collected in to a Volume, I engage to pay the said Thomas Percy \or his Executors/ the sum of twenty ten guineas as soon as a thousand \copies/ of the said Volume are sold off and not before, after which he is to have no farther demands for the same on me, Witness my hand this 21 st day of May 1761.

Ja^s Dodsley'

Wawn (2000, 27) points out that the word 'Runic' in the title is corrected from 'Punic', and comments: 'If "Punic" was Dodsley's accident, "Five" may have been partly his design, for Percy was prevented from including several additional pieces to the five actually published in 1763.' Possibly so, though Percy's letter to Shenstone of September 1760, quoted below, indicates that he himself was thinking of a small volume corresponding to Macpherson's *Fragments of Ancient Poetry Collected in the Highlands of Scotland*.

[2] Percy's friend and mentor William Shenstone upbraided him for the delay in a

The delay seems not to have been caused by any one thing, but rather to have come about through a conjunction of several factors, including the complexity of the task of preparing the Old Norse poems for the edition, which he may not have bargained for when he began, and the fact that he was working on other projects in the years 1761-3, particularly his major work *Reliques of Ancient English Poetry*, which took up a lot of his time and was not published until 1765.

Although his later work on Old Norse-Icelandic literature, *Northern Antiquities*, achieved wide popularity with the British reading public for at least a century and went through three editions (1770, 1809 and 1847), *Five Pieces of Runic Poetry* was not so popular in terms of its publication history. However, it attracted a number of reviews and imitations in the literary periodicals, and these have been listed by Amanda Collins in Table 1 of Clunies Ross 1998, 237. As she writes (Collins in Clunies Ross 1998, 209), 'the series of English translations and paraphrases of such Old Norse poems as *Krákumál* and *The Incantation of Hervor* ... that found their way into eighteenth-century literary periodicals is a testimony to the seminal role played by *Northern Antiquities* and Percy's earlier work *Five Pieces of Runic Poetry* in the dissemination and popularisation of Northern myth and poetry.' If imitation is the sincerest form of flattery, Percy's Norse translations, together with those of Thomas Gray,[3] were very successful and can be seen to have triggered a fashion in British literary circles for Old Norse poetry, alongside the passion for early Celtic verse aroused by James Macpherson's publication between 1760-3 of the poetry of the supposedly fourth-century Scottish bard Ossian. I have discussed the intellectual and literary background to all these works in *The Norse Muse in Britain, 1750-1820* (1998), to which the reader is referred for a fuller discussion. The four Tables in that book on pp. 237-72, compiled by Amanda Collins, show

---

small postscript to a letter dated October 1761: 'How happens it, I beseech you, that you have suppressed the *Runick Fragments &c* 'till Mr. McPherson has published *His* Poem? [viz. *Fingal*] Why will you suffer the Publick to be quite *cloyed* with the kind of writing, ere you avail yourself of their *Appetite*? I cannot say whether you should *now* defer the publication, or publish directly.' (BL MS Add. 28221, f. 79r, Brooks 1977, 124).

[3] Thomas Gray's Norse translations were *The Descent of Odin*, based on the eddic poem *Baldrs Draumar*, and *The Fatal Sisters*, based on *Darraðarljóð*. These translations were completed by 1761 but not published until 1768. For a more detailed discussion and comparison with Percy's work, see Clunies Ross 1998 and Wawn 2000, 29-30.

clearly both the spate of publications, many of them in the literary magazines, inspired by Gray's and Percy's work, and the interesting fact that through most of the second part of the eighteenth century the Old Norse poems translated by British men and women remained the small, and in many ways atypical, selection that Percy had first published in 1763.

The five poems included in *Five Pieces* were, in the order in which they were presented, and as Percy entitled them, *The Incantation of Hervor*, now usually termed in English *The Waking of Angantyr*, from *Hervarar saga*; *The Dying Ode of Regner Lodbrog*, that is, *Krákumál*; *The Ransome of Egill the Scald*, now known as Egill Skallagrímsson's *Hǫfuðlausn*; *The Funeral Song of Hacon* or *Hákonarmál*; and *The Complaint of Harold*, six stanzas attributed to Haraldr harðráði and supposedly addressed to Ellisif, daughter of Prince Jarizleifr of Kiev. These verses were widely understood as a love poem in the eighteenth century, and as evidence that the bloodthirsty Vikings were also capable of gentler passions. Aside from the last-mentioned poem, all the others were presented by Percy as examples of the heroic genre of *epicedium* or funeral ode and illustrated the claim he made in his Preface to *Five Pieces* that 'the poetry of the Scalds chiefly displays itself in images of terror. Death and war were their favourite subjects, and in expressions on this head their language is amazingly copious and fruitful.'

Percy's sources for this selection of Old Norse poetry were some of the most influential works of seventeenth-century Scandinavian scholarship in Old Norse studies. He found *The Incantation of Hervor* in Olaus Verelius's 1672 edition of *Hervarar Saga på Gammal Götska*, and also in Thomas Bartholin's *Antiquitates Danicae*, published in Copenhagen in 1689. However, the chief source for his English translation of this poem was George Hickes' *Thesaurus* (1703-5). Bartholin's influential account of the ancient Scandinavians' stoical scorn of death and their heroic bravery combined speculative ethnography with plentiful citation of Old Norse texts, both prose and poetry, many of them previously unknown to non-Icelanders. The examples were obtained for Bartholin by his assistant, Árni Magnússon, who is better known as a manuscript collector and scholar in his own right (Bekker-Nielsen and Widding 1972). *Antiquitates Danicae* was in fact one of the most important means whereby reliable Icelandic texts with facing Latin translations were disseminated in Europe. Percy found *The Complaint of Harold* in Bartholin, and also discovered quotations from all the other poems in *Five Pieces* there, though he did not use Bartholin as his chief source for these. His main source for *The Dying Ode of Regner Lodbrog* was Ole Worm's *Literatura Runica*, published in 1636, and this is where he also found *The Ransome of Egill the Scald*. The remaining source, for *The Funeral Song of Hacon*, was Johan Peringskiöld's 1697 edition of Snorri Sturluson's *Heimskringla*, and we shall see that he took other poetic material from here too, though it was never published. Most of these works had the important advantage to the scholar with little or no knowledge of Icelandic, that they provided facing Latin translations of the Norse texts. They are discussed in greater detail in Clunies Ross 1998, 75-84.

The indirect influence of *Five Pieces of Runic Poetry* upon British literary tastes did not lead to the independent publication of a second or later edition. However, the second edition of *Northern Antiquities* which appeared in two volumes in Edinburgh in 1809, shortly before Percy's death in 1811, contained a reprint of *Five Pieces* as an appendix to the second volume (pp. 279-328) with a slightly altered Preface. The fact that this influential little book has never been independently republished, together with the existence of a number of translations of Old Norse poetry that Percy made at about the same time as he was working on *Five Pieces* but which for the most part have never been published, have led me to the present project. I decided to produce a facsimile edition of the 1763 work, together with my own notes, and, in addition, an edition of the unpublished translations. These are all in a scrapbook of Percy's notes and rough drafts in the Bodleian Library, Oxford, MS Percy c. 7. This manuscript contains a number of draft translations of Norse poems and other fragments relating to Norse subjects on ff. 1-44 (some of which are pertinent to the material in *Five Pieces*), while the rest of the manuscript, headed 'Spanish Romances' (f. 45r ff.), contains his draft translations for *Ancient Songs Chiefly on Moorish Subjects*, a project that was also never published in his lifetime (Nichol Smith 1932).

The translations in the notebook are of considerable significance to modern scholarship for several reasons.[4] First, they show that Percy was interested in a much wider range of poetry than is obvious from *Five Pieces*; they also reveal a good deal about his working methods; and they

---

[4] To J. A. W. Bennett in his excellent Oxford D. phil. thesis of 1938, pp. 256-8 (unfortunately never published – it was before its time) belongs the credit for first recognising and recording the importance of this material; see also Clunies Ross 1998, 96 and Wawn 2000, 26-7.

are of importance to modern scholars who have developed an interest in the history of their discipline and in the reception of Old Norse-Icelandic poetry after the Middle Ages and beyond the shores of Iceland. They are of particular significance for a study of how people outside Iceland came to appreciate skaldic poetry and the difficulties that lay in their way. They show Percy as undeterred though sometimes hampered by the problems of interpretation that skaldic verse presents, with its often fractured syntax and elaborate diction. They also show him trying to make as close a translation of his Icelandic originals as his relative lack of knowledge of the language would allow and the Latin translations of his sources would permit. The nature of the kenning posed problems of particular difficulty for early translators, as indeed it does today, though our knowledge of how this metalinguistic system worked is much superior to that of people in the eighteenth century. Percy's evident interest in skaldic poetry was quite unusual in his day,[5] and indeed for much of the time before the last fifty years, so there is considerable value in publishing the translations in his notebook at the present time, when scholars are preparing a new edition of the corpus of skaldic poetry[6] and there is also much interest in the reception of Old Norse literature in Britain and in other parts of Europe.[7]

It is almost certainly because Percy was somewhat out of step with the tastes of his age that he did not publish the translations in Bodley Percy c. 7. The story of how at least some of these translations were vetoed by Percy's friend William Shenstone is a dramatic one and indicative of the kinds of pressures that conservative contemporary tastes could exert upon a desire to innovate in literature.[8] There is very strong circumstantial

---

[5] A good deal of information about the attitudes of Percy's own day and later can be found in Clunies Ross 1998, 94-6, 192-3, 200-2, 203-5 and 224. See also Wawn 2000, 289 and 349. Even towards the end of the eighteenth century, enthusiasts for Old Norse literature such as Sir Walter Scott and William Herbert, translator of a good deal of eddic poetry, denounced skaldic verse as obscure and decadent. Cf. also Frank 1985 for a survey of changing attitudes to skaldic poetry.

[6] See Margaret Clunies Ross, Kari Gade, Edith Marold, Guðrún Nordal and Diana Whaley, *Norse-Icelandic Skaldic Poetry of the Scandinavian Middle Ages. Editors' Manual.* Centre for Medieval Studies, University of Sydney, July 2000.

[7] For a survey of recent research, see Clunies Ross and Lönnroth 1999 and, for Britain in particular, Clunies Ross 1998 and Wawn 2000.

[8] I have discussed the evidence for Shenstone's intervention to dissuade Percy from publishing skaldic verses in Clunies Ross 1998, 72-3. William Shenstone (1714-1763) was a minor poet and essayist and leader of a literary circle that used to meet

evidence that Percy's first attempts at translating Old Norse poetry took place about September 1760, when he sent a letter to William Shenstone, almost certainly enclosing a translation of *Hákonarmál*, entitled *The Epicedium of Haco*, together with a *lausavísa* (single stanza) by the Norwegian skald Þjóðólfr of Hvinir, and two stanzas from Eyvindr skáldaspillir's *Háleygjatal*, both of which are printed in this volume among Percy's other unpublished translations from the works of Viking Age skalds. The main part of the letter has been printed in Cleanth Brooks' edition of the Percy-Shenstone correspondence[9] (1977, 70-1, no. XXIV), but the two other translations, which were included with the letter as a postscript, were not published until 1988. Margaret Smith (1988) has demonstrated convincingly that Shenstone vetoed the publication of the two fragments, and that the postscript containing them is one and the same as the present f. 2r and v of MS Bodley Percy c. 7. A portion of the text still bears Shenstone's firm note of rejection, 'I think not by any means', to Percy's question about whether it would be worthwhile to include such 'smaller fragments' in 'our Collection'. Margaret Smith (1988, 476) thought Percy was suggesting here that the 'smaller fragments' might be included with the material Percy was compiling towards what was to become *Reliques of Ancient English Poetry*, and that remains a possibility, even though *Reliques* contained no non-English verses, except for two Spanish poems at the end of Volume 1. I have suggested (1998, 54, note 12 and 72) that he may possibly have meant the collection of poems, by Shenstone and various of his literary friends, now referred to as *Shenstone's Miscellany*, and published as late as 1952 by Ian Gordon. This did contain translations from exotic languages, including some supplied by Percy from Spanish and Chinese but not Norse.

---

at his rural retreat, The Leasowes, in Worcestershire. Percy frequently discussed his translations from 'ancient poetry' with Shenstone, both by letter and in person, and was a contributor to a miscellany volume (ed. Gordon 1952) which was put together from the compositions and translations of Shenstone's circle to exemplify their literary tastes for simplicity and 'natural' language.

[9] Now BL MS Add. 28221, *Correspondence between Rev. T. Percy and W. Shenstone 1757-1763*; the letter in question is on ff. 48r-49v. Percy compiled this set of letters between himself and Shenstone at some time after the latter's death on 11 February 1763 and has annotated it in a number of places. He presumably removed the postscript from the letter of September 1760 and at some time placed it with his other unpublished translations and drafts in what is now Bodley MS Percy c. 7.

Thomas Percy as a Translator of Old Norse Poetry

In the body of the letter to Shenstone of September 1760, Percy explained that he had a new translation project in hand, and one that was distinct from the collection of material for *Reliques* that the two men had been discussing and continued to discuss over several years. He wrote:

> 'Inclosed I send you an ancient Celtic, (or rather Runic) Poem, translated from the Icelandic.[10] I am making up a small Collection of Pieces of this kind for the Press, which will be about the Size of the Erse Fragments. You will probably be disgusted to see it so incumbered with Notes; Yet some are unavoidable, as the Piece would be unintelligible without them.
>
> Some Passages in the inclosed seem to border upon Fustian and Bombast, but we must allow for the difference between a Version and an Original. Many things may seem overstrained in the former, which are natural and easy enough in the latter. Many Metaphors are to be found in all languages Which have been rendered familiar and easy by Use; but would appear forced and unnatural if they were to be resolved into their Primary Ideas.
>
> I send you also some smaller Fragments of the same kind: Give me your opinion, whether you think them worth inserting; as also whether I should print the originals; which after all nobody will understand.'[11]

We see in this letter a number of Percy's characteristic attitudes to the

---

[10] Percy has inserted an asterisk here and, on the facing blank page (f. 48v) has added, at a later date, presumably when annotating the correspondence after Shenstone's death, the following words: 'Afterwards printed in Five Pieces of Runic Poetry, translated from the Icelandic & published by Dodsley 1764 [*sic*] 8vo'. The 'ancient Celtic (or rather Runic) Poem' was very likely *Hákonarmál* (Clunies Ross 1998, 72-3) and see also notes to this poem below. *Hákonarmál*, like the fragments Shenstone rejected, was translated from Johan Peringskiöld's edition of Snorri Sturluson's *Heimskringla*.

[11] I cite the text here from the ms, BL MS Add. 28221, f. 49r. It is printed by Brooks 1977, 70-1 with a few very small differences.

translator's task well displayed, as well as his obvious awareness that Shenstone was not likely to condone so many notes as Percy rightly believed would be needed to explain these poems to an ignorant public. He also signalled his inclination, as a scholar, to include the originals, even if no one could understand them. In a letter dated October 1, 1760, Shenstone responded more or less in the manner Percy had anticipated, although with some appreciation of the longer poem, probably *The Funeral Song of Hacon*:

> 'With Regard to the Celtic Poem, I think there is something *good* in it – The absolute *Necessity* of Notes, will be the Rock that you may chance to split upon. I hope they will be as short as possible, & either at the end of every *Piece*; or thrown into the Form of Glossary at the end of the *Collection*. Perhaps some small Preface at the Beginning also, may supersede the Use of *Many* – I would rather chuse to have the translation be a kind of *flowing* yet *pompous Prose*; & printed in *Paragraphs* accordingly – The Original, I should think, had much better be omitted; partly for the Reasons you give yourself; and partly, lest this, *together with* the Notes, may *load* the text more than is agreeable. I should be glad enough to revise, *with you*, this whole Collection when tis put together; In the mean time, I would not trouble you to send me each particular Piece; as it is very probable I shall not have means to afford you much assistance.
>
> A Question of yours remains with regard to the *smaller* Fragments of the Celtick Poetry – There should be *certainly* nothing of this kind inserted, that is *less* considerable than what you send me; And as to these, and a *Few* of the Kind, they, perhaps, may not be much exceptionable. However, if it be the least necessary to add *notes* by way of *explanation*, the<n one> may readily enough conclude that they had better all be totally *omitted*.'[12]

Percy was in the habit of taking Shenstone's advice to heart, and there can be no doubt that he carried out a number of the suggestions made in this letter. In *Five Pieces* his translations were in prose and printed in

---

[12] BL MS Add. 28221, f. 51r, Brooks 1977, 74.

paragraphs, while the 'smaller Fragments' were suppressed.[13] On the other hand, although there was a 'small Preface at the Beginning', there was also an Introduction to each poem, and there was a select number of notes to the translations at the foot of the pages on which they were printed. And at the end of the volume, 'The Islandic Originals of the preceding Poems' appeared, together with an acknowledgement of Percy's sources for them. He even managed to squeeze in a couple of the forbidden short fragments in the guise of notes to the longer poems, and their 'originals' are also printed at the end of the book. By the time *Five Pieces* was published, Shenstone was dead (he died on 11 February 1763), but the volume, when it appeared a few months later, was probably something of a compromise between Percy's own inclinations, a desire to follow Shenstone's advice, and the intention to provide a scholarly counter to the dubious authenticity of James Macpherson's extremely successful 'Erse Fragments'. This is a major reason why Percy included the 'Islandic Originals', as he made clear in his Preface. The status of *Five Pieces* as a riposte and counter-weight to Macpherson is everywhere apparent in its design (cf. Clunies Ross 1998, 59-70).

Another of the Percy-Shenstone letters reveals that Percy was by no means insensitive to the literary appeal of Macpherson's translations, even though he disliked their turgidity and affectation and, like many others, suspected their authenticity. In a letter to Shenstone of 22 February 1762, Percy tells his friend:

> 'I am reading *Fingal*. – I wish the Translator had had Mr.
> Shenstone's Ear: or rather Mr. Shenstone himself at his
> elbow. You would have found some other things to have
> altired, beside the flow of his prose. There is too little
> simplicity of narration: all is thrown into metaphor &
> sentence: the latter too often affected & stiff: the former too
> frequently turgid & harsh. An affectation of Erse Idiom is too
> generally studied: so as to betray (I think) a consciousness
> that the piece is not what it is made to pass for. – After all it
> is a most extraordinary production, whether modern or
> antique; richly abounds both with sublime & pathetic: &
> shews a Genius in the Composer equal to any Epic

---

[13] The fact that in his ms notebook the smaller fragments appear as free verse indicates that his inclination was probably to present all his translations in that way.

production.'[14]

This shrewd assesment of Macpherson's work also reveals something of Percy's own attitude to the process of translation, doubtless influenced by Shenstone. Although he recognised that older poetry frequently contained complex metaphors, as he makes clear in the Preface to *Five Pieces* and in his letter to Shenstone of September 1760, quoted above, he was inclined to simplicity and austerity of narration where these were possible. In a number of his own translations he achieves this objective by following the Latin translations of his 'Islandic Originals' closely. As they are frequently denuded of the metaphorical richness of the Old Norse, since they tend not to translate kennings and other common Norse poetic figures fully or at all, Percy was often saved from the necessity to avoid turgidity and harshness or 'Fustian and Bombast', as he terms it in the letter. On the other hand, he probably felt that some judicious touch of authentic Old Norse imagery was both decorative and desirable,[15] and his translations from time to time include literal renditions of some of the less florid kennings, with appropriate explanatory notes. The remarks on Macpherson's style also reveal a distaste for 'sentence' and an 'affectation of Erse Idiom'. By contrast, Percy is a self-effacing translator and certainly one who chooses a plain unmarked idiom for the most part, unlike both Macpherson and Thomas Gray, whose Norse translations are full of verbal allusions to the classics of English and Latin literature.

Percy's last comment on Macpherson is also pertinent to an assessment of his own role as a translator of Old Norse poetry. Notwithstanding his criticisms of the detail, he appreciates Macpherson's production as a whole; it 'richly abounds both with sublime & pathetic'. In his own work considered as a whole, though it is austere, one cannot escape the impression that he enjoyed and appreciated Old Norse poetry, and was not deterred by apparent obscurity or difficulty in his sources. As a good number of the Norse poems he translated were in skaldic measures or, if in eddic verse-forms, ones often classified along with skaldic poetry by modern scholars - *Hákonarmál* and *Darraðarljóð*, for example - this alone

---

[14] BL MS Add. 28221, f. 90r and v, Brooks 1977, 141-2.

[15] This attitude was shared in part by Thomas Gray (cf. Clunies Ross 1998, 111), but Gray's amplification of a small number of powerful images in his translations was far more literary and in the *ut pictura poesis* tradition, which Percy did not use at all.

is a measure of his openness to the Norse poetic corpus. He did not come to it with a prejudgement about the quality of any of its parts. This characteristic of Percy as translator becomes much more apparent when we are able to study the previously unpublished material in Bodleian MS Percy c. 7, as almost all of it is skaldic, and some in the chief skaldic measure of *dróttkvætt*.

Taken together, the four sets of verses Percy translated from *Heimskringla* (in addition to *Hákonarmál*) provide an excellent introduction to Norwegian and Icelandic skaldic poetry of the late ninth and tenth centuries. They include a *lausavísa* by Þjóðólfr of Hvinir, five stanzas from the *Haraldskvæði* of Þorbjǫrn hornklofi, four stanzas from Eyvindr Finnsson skáldaspillir's *Háleygjatal*, and five stanzas from Einarr Helgason skálaglamm's *Vellekla*. Had they been published in the eighteenth century, they would have given the discerning reader a pretty accurate idea of the nature of skaldic court poetry of the Viking Age, for the verses include both *lofkvæði* (encomium) and genealogical poetry, as well as a sample of the occasional *lausavísa*. These skaldic translations are far less influenced by contemporary blood and guts ideas of Viking Age society and its poetry than are the poems included in *Five Pieces of Runic Poetry*, and it was doubtless for this reason, and because Shenstone had come down so heavily against them, that Percy refrained from publishing them. However, the mere existence of the Bodleian manuscript scrapbook and the fact that he must have inserted the rejected fragments into it at some time after he had come into possession of his deceased friend's correspondence with him, shows that Percy privately valued skaldic poetry, unlike almost all his contemporaries and most other scholars and literary people for the following two hundred years.

Not only did Percy actually like this sort of poetry – he talks of a 'beautiful fragment of an ancient runic poem' on f. 4v of the Bodleian manuscript – but he also had a shrewd understanding of how skaldic verses were used in Old Norse prose historiography and thus of the context of their preservation in medieval Icelandic manuscripts. In the postscript to the letter in which Shenstone vetoed his 'smaller fragments', Percy explains that it will be difficult to find many 'Celtic' [*sic*] pieces 'so well preserved & so intire as *the Epicedium of Haco*; or *the Incantation of Hervor*' because of the nature of the preservation of this poetry in 'some of the Old Gothic Prose Histories' where verses tended to be 'inserted as Vouchers to Facts'. This rather sophisticated understanding of what has recently been termed the 'authenticating' type of verse quotation (cf. Whaley 1993a), would not disgrace a modern scholar. In the same postscript he also shows his awareness of the nature of the *lausavísa* as 'independent and detached'.

To judge by Percy's other activities as a translator and editor, most notably of *Reliques of Ancient English Poetry*, but also of literature from a variety of languages, his natural inclination was to be scholarly, though his extremely wide-ranging interests and the speed with which he normally worked would have precluded great depth of learning and research in any one area. In September 1760, when he first wrote to Shenstone about his idea of putting together a small collection of 'runic' poems for the press, he probably expected to accomplish the task relatively quickly. That he did not do so, can be attributed to many factors including the difficulty of obtaining suitable poems (cf. Clunies Ross 1998, 53-8), but one of the most important reasons for the unexpected complexity of the task probably lay in Percy's close contact with his near neighbour Edward Lye. Percy came to live in Northamptonshire, as vicar of the parish of Easton Maudit, in 1756. Only one and a half miles from Easton was the neighbouring village of Yardley Hastings, where Edward Lye was rector. Although he was a country clergyman, Lye was probably the most able English scholar of his day in the field of comparative Germanic languages and, by the time Percy met him, had already published two substantial books, an English etymological dictionary, based on manuscripts compiled by Franciscus Junius in the seventeenth century, and an edition of the Codex Argenteus, the Gothic Gospels in the library of Uppsala University in Sweden.[16] Lye was a scholar more of Anglo-Saxon and Gothic than Old Norse, but he certainly knew the rudiments of Old Icelandic grammar and seems to have had a reasonable knowledge of the literature as well. He had many contacts in

---

[16] On Lye see Clunies Ross 1999 and Clunies Ross and Collins forthcoming. His two publications were *Francisci Junii Francisci Filii Etymologicum Anglicanum. Ex autographo descripsit et accessionibus permultis auctum edidit Edwardus Lye A. M. Ecclesiæ Parochialis de Yardley-Hastings in agro Northamptoniensi Rector. Præmittuntur vita auctoris et Grammatica anglo-saxonica.* (Oxonii: E Theatro Sheldoniano, 1743) and *Sacrorum Evangeliorum Versio Gothica ex Codice Argenteo Emendata atque Suppleta, cum Interpretatione Latina & Annotationibus Erici Benzelii non ita pridem Archiepiscopi Upsaliensis.* Edidit, Observationes suas Adjecit, Et Grammaticam Gothicam Præmisit Edwardus Lye A. M. (Oxonii, E Typographeo Clarendoniano, MDCCL.) Imprimatur, J. Purnell, Febr. 19. 1749 Vice-Can. Oxon.

Sweden and it was partly through them that he was able to amass a very good library of Scandinavian books by eighteenth-century standards, which he lent to Percy as required. It also appears from Percy's unpublished diary that the two men visited each other frequently, sometimes on a daily basis. From the evidence of the diary, their letters and extant notes in Lye's hand among Percy's books and manuscripts, Lye seems to have taken charge of Percy's education in Old Norse-Icelandic studies and insisted on going through his translations with him.[17] Such contact doubtless delayed the production of copy for *Five Pieces* because Lye would have made Percy aware of as many of the linguistic complexities of the task as he himself knew about and is unlikely to have let mistakes slip past without correction.

By modern standards, Percy's Norse translations are far from perfect and usually rely on the parallel Latin versions that accompanied the Icelandic texts of most seventeenth- and eighteenth-century editions of medieval Norse literature. As the Latin translations were usually the work of Icelanders, these are tolerably accurate for the most part, though sometimes they only give the general sense of a verse rather than an exact translation. However, Percy's translations are not simply English versions of these Latin texts. In *Five Pieces*, we find evidence of an independent view and of considerable reading in the subject of medieval Scandinavian culture, both in the Introductions to each poem, the presentation of the 'Islandic originals' and in the textual notes, some of which are unfortunately based on false or misleading information. For a few of the notes, Percy is indebted to Lye; for the introductory material, he often takes inspiration from Paul-Henri Mallet's *Introduction á l'Histoire de Dannemarc* (1755) and *Monuments de la Mythologie et de la Poésie des Celtes* (1756), which he owned. He acquired a copy of the second edition of Mallet when it came out in 1763, and his decision to translate Mallet, and augment it considerably with his own critical notes and translations in *Northern Antiquities* may be seen as a logical extension of the work he did towards *Five Pieces* (Clunies Ross 1994).

William Shenstone would not have approved of the present edition of Thomas Percy's translations from Old Norse poetry. For one thing it

---

[17] For Percy's diary, see entries in BL MS Add. 32336, *Memoranda of Bishop Percy*, Vol. 1, 1753-1778; for Percy-Lye correspondence, see Clunies Ross and Collins forthcoming, and for Lye's handwritten notes, see Clunies Ross 1998, 58. There are notes in Lye's hand to some of the poems Percy translated in Bodley MS Percy c. 7 on ff. 36-39.

publishes the fragments he vetoed, and, for another, it adds even more notes to Percy's original comments! For a modern readership, however, particularly one interested in Percy's approach to the project of translation and the difficulties he faced, the newly published texts and additional notes allow us to understand his working methods, the extent of his knowledge and the nature of the editions and translations he worked from. A comparison between what modern scholarship considers the best manuscripts and the most likely readings of the difficult texts he translated and his own renditions, as well as those of the editions he worked from, reveals a lot about the reception history of Old Norse poetry, particularly skaldic poetry. One of the most interesting findings of such a comparison is that no one at that time had devised a method for translating skaldic kennings in order to bring out the full meaning, often metaphorical, of this kind of poetry. This may have been partly a matter of convention and a response to contemporary taste rather than an inability to perform the task. Those Icelanders who understood the kennings and could translate them fully appear to have followed a convention of expressing only the kenning's referent and not the periphrastic kenning itself in their Latin and modern Scandinavian renditions. This is likely to have been, at least in part, a response to the distaste of their mainland Scandinavian patrons for over-complex diction, but it effectively robbed the poetry of much of its meaning. The first translators of Old Icelandic poetry into English to have overcome this problem were Grímur Jónsson Thorkelín and James Johnstone in their edition of *Krákumál, Lodbrokar-Quida*, in 1782.[18]

---

[18] The edition was issued under Johnstone's name, though it was the work of both men: James Johnstone, 1782, *Lodbrokar-Quida; or The Death-Song of Lodbrog; now first correctly printed from various Manuscripts, with a free English translation. To which are added the various readings; a literal Latin version; an Islando-Latino glossary; and explanatory notes*. Printed for the Author, n. p. For a discussion of the genesis of this translation, see Clunies Ross 1998, 173-179.

A Chronology of Percy's Translations of Old Norse Poetry and Related Events

1760

June, James Macpherson publishes anonymously at Edinburgh *Fragments of Antient Poetry, Collected in the Highlands of Scotland, and translated from the Galic or Erse Language.*

September, Percy writes to William Shenstone, the letter retrospectively dated by him 'Sepr. ... 1760' (BL Add. 28221, f. 49r; Brooks 1977, 70): 'Inclosed I send you an ancient Celtic, (or rather Runic) Poem, translated from the Icelandic. I am making up a small Collection of Pieces of this kind for the Press, which will be about the size of the Erse Fragments.' Shenstone tolerates the whole poem but rejects the fragments.

[The specimens were probably an early version of *The Funeral Song of Hacon*, a *lausavísa* by Þjóðólfr of Hvinir (*Translations from the works of Viking Age skalds* No. 1.1) and the first two verses of No. 1.2, stanzas 6-7 of Eyvindr skáldaspillir's *Háleygjatal*, all taken from Peringskiöld's edition of *Heimskringla*]

1761

May 21, Percy obtains a signed agreement from James Dodsley (now Bodleian MS Eng. Lett. d. 59, f. 8r) to publish '*five* pieces of *Runic Poetry translated from the Islandic Language*'. His diary entry for this day (BL MS Add. 32336, f. 24v) records 'Bargained with dodsley for Solomon's Song & Runic Poetry'.

July 3, Percy returns Francis Wise's *Enquiries concerning the First Inhabitants ... of Europe* (1758) to Edward Lye (Bodleian MS Percy c. 9, f. 99r)

July 11, Percy returns *Dryden's Miscellany* and Ole Worm's *Literatura Runica* to Lord Sussex's library (Bodleian MS Percy c. 9, f. 95v)

mid-1761, Percy returns Edward Lye's copy of 'Snorro Sturleson fol.' (probably Peringskiöld's *Heimskringla*) to him. (Bodleian MS Percy c. 9, f. 99v)

July 21, Percy writes to Evan Evans, 'I have prevailed on a friend to attempt a Translation of some ancient Runic Odes composed among the snows of Norway, which will make their appearance at Mr Dodsley's shop next winter' (BL MS Add. 32330, f. 12r; Lewis 1957, 3) Percy also refers to the impending publication in letters to Evans of 15 October and November 1761 (Lewis 1957, 21 and 23).

October 3, Percy borrows Ole Worm's *Monumenta Danorum* from Lord Sussex (returns it 14 August 1762) (Bodleian MS Percy c. 9, f. 95v)

after December 1-3, Shenstone writes to Percy, immediately after Macpherson's publication of *Fingal*, to upbraid him for being so slow in producing *Five Pieces*: 'How happens it, I beseech you, that you have suppressed the *Runick Fragments* &c 'till Mr. McPherson has published *His* Poem?' (BL MS Add. 28221 f.79r; Brooks 1977, 124).

December 19, Edward Lye invites Percy to dine with him and check his translation of *Krákumál*: 'To understand the Icelandic Poetry, one ought to have their Edda at our fingers ends. I have gone thro Lodbrog, and desire You wou'd come and dine with me on Monday, that we run it over together' (BL MS Add. 32325, f. 179r). [At some unspecified date Percy had borrowed 'L'Edda. Island. & Lat. 4to.' from Lye, probably Resen's 1664 edition. Lye received from a Swedish friend a copy of Göransson's 1746 edition of *Snorra Edda*, which Percy later used for *Northern Antiquities*, in June 1764 (BL MS Add. 32325, ff. 213r-214v).]

1762

March 26, Percy receives his own copy of Bartholin's *Antiquitates Danicae* from the bookseller Tonson (Bodleian MS Percy c. 9, f. 97v).

April 30, Percy returns Lye's copy of *Hervarar saga* (Verelius's edition), the entry underneath itemising 'Hickes's Thesaurus', but not giving a date of return (Bodleian MS Percy c. 9, f. 99r).

July 25, Percy writes to Evan Evans in a letter that 'contains some specimens of Runic Poetry: The two printed sheets are part of a small collection that will make its appearance at Mr Dodsley's shop next winter' (Lewis 1957, 26-7). The specimens referred to are likely to have been fair copies of *The Complaint of Harold* and a stanza by Rǫgnvaldr kali on his accomplishments, which appears in a Postscript to the former in *Five Pieces* (pp. 80-1). These drafts are now in the National Library of Wales, as

MS Panton 74, f. 109a-d.

August 14, Percy tells Evans 'As the Five Pieces of Runic Poetry will be fit for publication towards Michaelmas: – I wish you would get ready such another Collection of British Poetry...' (BL MS Add. 32330, f. 39 r & v; Lewis 1957, 30)

October 10, Percy writes again to Evans: 'Inclosed I send you two more sheets of Runic Poetry, and will transmit the rest as fast as they come from the press' (Lewis 1957, 40).

November 28, Percy to Evans: 'But I would not defer sending you the inclosed. [an unidentified sheet or sheets of *Five Pieces*] – The Title-page and Preface to the Runic Poetry are not yet printed off; when they are I will transmit them' (Lewis 1957, 45).

1763

February 11, death of William Shenstone

April 14, Percy publishes *Five Pieces of Runic Poetry* with R. and J. Dodsley in Pall Mall.

April, Percy writes to Evans: 'We have at length compleated our small Runic Publication; My Preface and Title-page I here inclose, begging the favour of you to prefix it to the Sheets formerly sent...' (Lewis 1957, 46-7).

April 30, Evans to Percy: 'I have received your Preface to your Runic Collection of poetry for which I am very much obliged to you' (Lewis 1957, 48).

May 8, Percy receives from the bookseller Newberry 'Mallet Hist. de Dannemarc 5 tom.' (Bodleian MS Percy c. 9, f. 98r). This was the second edition of *Mallet's Introduction á l'histoire de Dannemarc*, 6 vols. (Geneva, 1763). Percy possessed the first edition, which came out in two parts in 1755 and 1756, though exactly when he received them is not known. His copies of these volumes, which he drew on for *Five Pieces*, are now Queen's University Belfast, Percy 288 (see, for details Clunies Ross 1998, 55 and notes 15 and 16). For *Northern Antiquities*, published in 1770, begun in late 1763 and probably finished c. 1767 (Clunies Ross 1994), Percy used both first and second editions of Mallet.

Introduction to the Facsimile Edition
Five Pieces of Runic Poetry

The present facsimile of the 1763 edition of Thomas Percy's *Five Pieces of Runic Poetry* has been reproduced from scanned images of a copy in the Rare Books Department of the University of Sydney's Fisher Library, RB 4663.36. My own commentary has been added alongside the original text in order to place Percy's translations and his own notes and commentary in the context of modern research on the post-medieval reception of Old Norse poetry. Notes relating to particular lines of text are numbered in the margin next to the relevant line.

The book is a slim octavo volume, measuring 18.3 x 11.3 cm., whose signature composition is as follows: A-G^8, H^2. The Title Page (A1r) and Preface occupy the first gathering and have no other page numbering aside from the signatures A2-4. Beginning with the title page of the first poem (B1r), *The Incantation of Hervor*, the remaining 100 pages are numbered using arabic numerals, though numbers do not appear on title pages of poems nor on the final, additional page (H2). The book's pagination may also be expressed as [xvi] 99 [1].

Contents: A1r title page, A1v explanatory note, A2r -A8v Preface, B1r-G1v text of translations, G2r-H2r The Islandic Originals, H2v Additional note.

Where page references are given in my notes to Percy's edition, these refer to the pagination of the 1763 edition, and not to the pagination of the present edition, unless otherwise specified.

In the preparation of this facsimile edition I have consulted Percy's own copy of *Five Pieces*, which is No. 598 in the Rare Books Library of The Queen's University, Belfast.

FIVE PIECES

OF

RUNIC POETRY

Tranflated from the

ISLANDIC LANGUAGE.

1.

BꜰR Ɪↀ ꓕꝐꞮꝃꞀ ꓬꞮꓷ Ᵽ.
ꞀꝐꞮꓡ ꓬꓕꞓRꝐ ✷ꓥꓷꓕꓕ.
✷ꓥꝐꓕ ꓬꓷꞮꝃ Ɪↀ Ꝋꓬ.

    ✳   ✳   ✳ *Egill's Ode.*

ꝄRꞮꓬꓥꓬ BꞮꓲR ꓲꝊBRꓷꝐꝄ
ꓥR BꞮꓥꝐꓥꞮꝊꓥꓬ ✷ꓥꓷꞀ.
ꓟꞮꝃꝄꝄꝄ Ꞁꓬꓷꓰ Ɪↀ Ꝅꓵꓲ .

               Regner's Ode.

———Populi, quos defpicit Arctos,
Felices errore fuo, quos ille timorum
Maximus haud urget leti metus : inde ruendi
In ferrum mens prona viris, animæque capaces
Mortis ; et ignavum redituræ parcere vitæ.

                      LUCAN.

L O N D O N:
Printed for R. and J. DODSLEY, in Pall-mall,
MD CC LXIII.

Percy's title page was made up to resemble the title page of James Macpherson's *Fragments of Ancient Poetry* (Edinburgh, 1760). Both works are anonymous and Percy's formula 'Translated from the Icelandic Language' parallels Macpherson's 'Collected in the Highlands of Scotland and translated from the Galic or Erse Language', with the difference that, whereas Macpherson's formula suggests collection from unspecified and possibly oral sources, Percy is able to point to the written sources for his translations, citing two of them in the runic script popularised by Ole Worm in his *Literatura Runica* (1636). Both Macpherson and Percy include a quotation from Lucan's *De Bello Civili*, describing the religious beliefs and customs of the barbarian Celts and Germani living in the furthest reaches of the Roman Empire. Percy's citation is from Book I, 458-62, with its reference to the Northern nations' fearlessness of death on account of their belief in reincarnation and the transmigration of souls: 'Without a doubt the people overlooked by Arctos are fortunate in their mistake, not to be oppressed by that greatest terror, fear of death. This explains their warriors' willingness to rush upon the sword, their spirits keen for death, and their belief that it is cowardly to spare a life which will return' (Braund 1992, 15). Lucan was a classical author whose popularity was considerably greater in the eighteenth century than it is today. For a more detailed comparison of Percy's and Macpherson's title pages, see Clunies Ross 1998, 59-64.

1. Percy selected several lines from each of Egill Skallagrímsson's *Hǫfuðlausn* ('The Ransome of Egill the Scald') and *Krákumál* ('The Dying Ode of Regner Lodbrog'), as he found them in the versions of these poems printed in runes in the appendix to Ole Worm's *Literatura Runica*, 'Literarum Runicarum in Poesi usum uberius declarans', pp. 197-239. The three lines from *Hǫfuðlausn* are, in the order presented, from stanzas 2/3 (*berk Óðins mjǫð*, 'I carry Óðinn's mead'), 16/4 (*skal mærð hvata*, 'I shall hasten with [my] praise') and 18/6 (*hugat mælik þar*, 'I speak there what I have thought'). The lines selected from *Krákumál* were among those that expressed what eighteenth-century readers regarded as key concepts in ancient Scandinavian culture. They are 25/5-6 (*drekkum bjór af bragði/ ór bjúgviðum hausa*, 'we shall soon drink beer from the curved trees of skulls [DRINKING HORNS]', this kenning being interpreted in Percy's day to mean 'we shall drink beer out of the skulls of our enemies', and Ragnarr's famous death-defying 29/8, *læjandi skalk deyja*, 'laughing I shall die'.

N. B. This litte tract was drawn
up for the press in the year 1761:
but the publication has been delayed by an accident.

The publication history of *Five Pieces of Runic Poetry* is discussed in the Introduction to this edition. Percy is somewhat disingenuous in suggesting that an accident delayed publication, but he was probably covering his back in case critics complained about how long it had taken him to produce a book which, by his own admission in the Preface, was occasioned by Macpherson's success with his 1760 publication of 'Erse fragments'.

PREFACE.

*T*HE *ancient inhabitants of the nor-*
thern parts of Europe are generally
known under no other character than
that of a hardy and unpolished race, who
subdued all the southern nations by dint
of courage and of numbers. Their va-
lour, their ferocity, their contempt of
death, and passion for liberty, form the
outlines of the picture we commonly draw
of them: and if we sometimes revere them
for that generous plan of government
which they every where established, we
cannot help lamenting that they raised
the fabric upon the ruins of literature
and the fine arts.

Yet is there one feature of their cha-
racter of a more amiable cast; which, tho'
not so generally known, no less belongs

Percy's Preface expresses many of the key ideas of his age about 'ancient', that is, medieval, poetry. His chief argument is that although the ancient Scandinavians were barbarous, aggressive and primitive peoples, they had a number of saving graces, the chief of these being their 'amazing fondness for poetry', which, he argues, was of central importance in early Norse society, a point on which modern scholarship agrees. Like the other Germanic or 'Gothic' peoples, too, their legal and political systems had long been held to uphold the civil liberties which were by contrast lacking in recent English and European societies (Smith 1987), and their supposed beliefs in reincarnation and the transmigration of souls were held to have led them to a 'contempt of death' that caused them to perform sublime deeds of heroism, which were held to be the chief subjects of their poetry (Percy claims that 'death and war were their favourite subjects'). Four of the five poems Percy selected for *Five Pieces* are represented as epicedia or funeral odes. In fact only *Krákumál*, the 'Dying Ode of Regner Lodbrog' is strictly speaking an oration of a hero who is facing death, 'The Incantation of Hervor' being a dialogue between a woman and her dead father, 'The Funeral Song of Hacon' a poem celebrating the last battle of King Hákon the Good of Norway and his reception after death in Valhalla, and 'The Ransome of Egill the Scald' being a clever, insincerely flattering poem the skald is supposed to have composed at York to free himself from the threat of death at the hands of King Eiríkr Bloodaxe. However, all have something to do with the twin themes of death and heroism, so could loosely come under the epicedium rubric. The fifth poem, 'The Complaint of Harold', illustrates another theme which both Percy and Paul-Henri Mallet promoted, of the ancient Scandinavians as the originators of the medieval romance genre (see Clunies Ross 1998, 45-7), a theme Percy was to enlarge upon in his version of Mallet, *Northern Antiquities* (1770), and combine in *Reliques of Ancient English Poetry* (1765) with his theory that Northern skalds and Celtic bards were the early medieval ancestors of the minstrel class of the high Middle Ages, who 'got their livelihood by singing verses to the harp at the houses of the great' (1765 I, xv).

Like Hugh Blair, both in his Preface to Macpherson's *Fragments of Ancient Poetry* (1760) and his *A Critical Dissertation on the Poems of Ossian* (1763), Percy emphasises here that the poetry of primitive societies 'serve[s] ... to unlock the treasures of native genius' and to 'present us with frequent sallies of bold imagination, and constantly afford matter for philosophical reflection by showing the workings of the human mind in its almost original state of nature.'

PREFACE.

to them : and that is, an amazing fondness for poetry.   It will be thought a
paradox, that the same people, whose furious ravages destroyed the last poor remains of expiring genius among the Ro-
mans, should cherish it with all possible
care among their own countrymen : yet
so it was.   At least this was the case
among the ancient Danes, and from the
similarity of their religion, manners, and
customs, is equally credible of the other
nations of Teutonic race.

The ancient inhabitants of Sweden,
Denmark and Norway retained their original manners and customs longer than
any other of the Gothic tribes, and brought
them down nearer to our own times.   The
remoteness of their situation rendered ac-
cess to them slow and difficult : nor was
it till the tenth and eleventh centuries that
                                        christi-

PREFACE.

1.

christianity had gained an establishment among them. Hence it is that we are better acquainted with the peculiarities of their character, and have more of their original compositions handed down to us, than of any other of the northern nations,

2.

Of these compositions a great multitude are extant, some of them in print, others preserved in MS in the libraries of the north. All of them demonstrate that poetry was once held there in the highest estimation. The invention of it was attributed to the gods, and ranked among the most valuable gifts conferred on mortals. Those that excelled in it, were distinguished by the first honours of the state : were constant attendants on their kings, and were often employed on the most important commissions. These bards were called by the

A 3   *signi-*

1. One of the most widely accepted views among eighteenth-century literary theorists was that authentic 'ancient poetry' was necessarily pagan. Christian poetry, even if it could be shown to be old, as was the case with Old English verse, was disregarded because it was monkish and literate and so devoid of the primitive wildness deemed appropriate to ancient verse (Warton 1774, Preface, vi). Here, Percy argues that the reason why we have a good deal of early Scandinavian poetry extant is because the Scandinavians remained pagan for longer than other European peoples. He goes on, having his cake and eating it, to draw attention to one of his trump cards against Macpherson, the fact that 'of these compositions a great multitude are extant' in written form, whether in print or in manuscript. He of course disregards the fact that the preservation of early Norse poetry in manuscript form took place in the Christian era.

2. Percy would have been aware of some of the riches of Scandinavian libraries through George Hickes's publication, in the second volume of his *Thesaurus* (1705, 310-15) of an annotated list of titles of some Old Icelandic manuscripts held in the Royal Library at Stockholm, which he had been sent by Johan Peringskiöld. His own researches, and Edward Lye's library, furnished him with a number of printed editions of Icelandic texts, some of which he drew on for the texts of the poems published in *Five Pieces*.

PREFACE.

significant name of SCALD, *a word which implies " a smoother or polisher of language." ** *

The LANGUAGE *in which their productions are preserved, .and which once prevailed pretty extensively in the north, is commonly called* ISLANDIC : *Iceland being the place where it was supposed to be spoken in the greatest purity, and where it is to this day in use. The Islandic is the mother of the modern Swedish and Danish tongues, in like manner as the Anglo-saxon is the parent of our English. Both these mother-tongues are dialects of the ancient Gothic or Teutonic; and of so near affinity, that, in the opinion of*

* SKALLD a depilando dicti videntur, quod rudem orationem tanquam evulsis pilis perpoliunt. *Torfæi Præfat. ad Orcades.*
   The name of BARD also [Isl. *Barda*] was not unknown among the Islandic poets.

                                                                    the

1. Percy quotes an etymology suggested for the Old Norse noun *skáld*, 'poet', used especially of a court poet, which was proposed by the Icelandic scholar Torfæus (Þormóður Torfason), in the Preface to his *Orcades* (1697), 'skalds seem to be so called from their smoothing of language, because they thoroughly polish a rough speech as if extracting javelins'. Although there is still debate about the etymology of 'skald' (or 'scald', the earlier spelling in English), modern scholarship does not support the one proposed here, suitable as it was to Percy's argument. The most commonly accepted etymology is that the word is probably cognate with Modern English *scold*, sb., 'an abusive or nagging person' (usually used of a woman, and a Norse loanword) which may, however, appear in the Middle English *Ormulum* 2192 in the Norse sense of a poet. (*OED*, *scold*, sb., sense 1; cf. Onions, *Oxford Dictionary of Etymology* 1966, 798). Percy's readers are unlikely to have been familiar with the term, even though Aylett Sammes (1676, 438) had used the term 'Scalders'. The *OED* (*skald*, *scald*) cites *Five Pieces* as the first recorded occurrence of the word in English. The term 'bard', on the other hand, would have been more familiar to eighteenth-century readers, even though their ideas of what a bard was are not likely to have been exact. Its use in English to refer to a Celtic poet dates from the fifteenth century (*OED*, *bard*, sense 1), though its application, as here, 'to the early versifying minstrels or poets of other nations, before the use of writing' (*OED*, *bard*, sense 3), dates from the seventeenth and particularly the eighteenth centuries. There is no support for an Icelandic noun *Barda* in this sense. Percy probably got this idea from Edward Lye's *Etymologicum Anglicanum* (1743, *sub Bard*, 'poeta'), which suggests an Icelandic cognate **bar*, 'frons' (garland), possibly a confusion with *barð*, n, 'beard, brim (e.g. of hat or helmet)'.

PREFACE.

*the learned, what was spoken in one of
them, was without much difficulty understood by those, who used the other. Hence
it is, that such as study the originals of
our own language have constantly found
it necessary to call in the assistance of this
ancient sister dialect.*

1.

The CHARACTERS, *in which this
language was originally written, were
called* RUNIC; *from an Islandic word
that signifies a* FURROW*. *As the ma-
terials used for writing in the first rude
ages were only wood or stone, the conve-
nience of sculpture required that the strokes
should run chiefly in strait lines; and the
resemblance to plowing suggested the ap-
pellation. The word Runic was at first
applied to the letters only; tho' later*

2.

* RYN *Sulcus.* Vid. Olaij Wormij Literat. Runica. 1636. 4to. p. 2, 3.

A 4   *writers*

1. Percy's elevation of Icelandic to the status of 'mother of the modern Swedish and Danish tongues' is of course incorrect, as Icelandic is a development from Norwegian that took place after the settlement of the island in the late ninth century. However, as Icelandic has preserved many features of Old Norse that have been modified in Modern Scandinavian languages, and as a large proportion of extant Old Norse literature is in Old Icelandic, Percy may be pardoned for his mistake. His desire to establish a parallel between Old Icelandic and Old English (Anglo-Saxon) as related 'mother-tongues' allows him then to stress the special, family relationship between the study of 'our own language' and 'this ancient sister dialect'. This theme appears as a *leitmotif* in *Northern Antiquities*, where Percy constantly draws attention to parallels between the English language and customs and those of medieval Scandinavia, the effect being to suggest to the reader that he or she, as an English-speaker, has a special affinity with early Norse literature and culture. Four out of the five poems in *Five Pieces* would have appealed to an English readership because they appeared to have some connection with England and English history. Much of the action of 'The Dying Ode of Regner Lodbrog' and 'The Ransome of Egill the Scald' took place in England, while the hero of 'The Funeral Song of Hacon' was brought up at the court of King Athelstan of England and the hero of 'The Complaint of Harold' was a king who fought his last battle at Stamford Bridge.

2. It was the Danish scholar Ole Worm (whose erroneous etymology of the word 'rune' as meaning *sulcus*, 'furrow', is quoted by Percy here) who was responsible for introducing the notion that all early Norse texts were written in runes in his *Literatura Runica* of 1636. This idea was extremely popular in the seventeenth century (Seaton 1935), but Percy's statement here that 'the word Runic was at first applied to the letters only; tho' later writers have extended it to the verses written in them' may indicate some uncertainty about Worm's thesis, even though he quotes specimens of 'runic' verses directly from Worm on his title page and calls his book *Five Pieces of Runic Poetry* (cf. *OED*, *runic*, sense 2a).

PREFACE.

*writers have extended it to the verses
written in them.*

*A few specimens of these are now of-
fered to the public. It would be as vain
to deny, as it is perhaps impolitic to mention, that this attempt is owing to the
success of the ERSE fragments. It is by
no means for the interest of this little
work, to have it brought into a comparison with those beautiful pieces, after
which it must appear to the greatest dif-
advantage. And yet till the Translator
of those poems thinks proper to produce
his originals, it is impossible to say whether they do not owe their superiority,
if not their whole existence entirely to
himself. The Editor of these pieces had
no such boundless field for licence. Every
poem here produced has been already published accompanied with a Latin or Swedish*

1. Percy does a rather skilful job of distancing himself from the dubious side of the Ossian poetry and the ongoing debate about its sources and their authenticity, while at the same time acknowledging its undoubted literary appeal and its role as the spur to his publication of *Five Pieces*. He expressed his views in more detail in his correspondence with his friend William Shenstone, and these are discussed in the Introduction.

PREFACE.

difb verfion ; by which every deviation would at once be detected. It behoved him therefore to be as exact as poffible. Sometimes indeed, where a fentence was obfcure, he hath ventured to drop it, and the afterifks which occur will denote fuch omiffions. Sometimes for the fake of perfpicuity it was neceffary to alter the arrangement of a period; and fometimes to throw in a few explanatory words: and even once or twice to fubflitute a more fimple ex-pr.ffion inftead of the complex and enig-matic phrafe of the original.

1.

For the reader muft be informed that the productions of the Iflandic poets, tho' quite original and underived, are far from being fo eafy and fimple as might be ex-pected: on the contrary, no compofitions abound with more laboured metaphors, or more ftudied refinements. A proof that

poetry

1. Percy's statement on the superiority of his sources, on the ground of their indisputable status as written texts, is part of his polemic against James Macpherson. His additional remarks about his own scholarly approach to the task of editing were probably aimed in the same direction, though they read a little ironically in the context of later accusations against him, mainly by Joseph Ritson, that he had played fast and loose with the texts of poems he included in *Reliques* (cf. Clunies Ross 1998, 70 and note 42).

PREFACE.

poetry had been cultivated among them
for many ages. That daring spirit and
vigour of imagination, which diftinguifh-
ed the northern warriors, naturally in-
clined them to bold and fwelling figures:
and as their mythology was grown very
extenfive and complicated, the frequent
allufions to it could not but be a great
fource of obfcurity to modern readers. It
was the conftant ftudy of the northern
Scalds *to lift their poetic ftyle as much*
as poffible above that of their profe. So
that they had at length formed to them-
felves in verfe a kind of new language *,
in which every idea was expreffed by a
peculiar term, never admitted into their
ordinary converfe. Some of thefe terms
are founded on their mythology or the fa-

---

* Called by them, after the manner of the ancient Greeks, *(Afom-maal,)* THE LANGUAGE OF
THE GODS.

                              bulous

1. Percy, like Hugh Blair, in his *A Critical Dissertation on the Poems of Ossian*, was aware of an apparent contradiction between the commonly held eighteenth-century notion that the language of ancient poetry, as the expression of a primitive society, must be 'easy and simple', and the fact that the poetry they were presenting to the public 'abound[ed] with ... metaphors' and other figures. Here Percy ascribes these 'studied refinements' to the great age of the poetic tradition in Scandinavia, to the 'daring spirit' of the northern warriors, and the extensiveness and complication of Northern mythology, for which is he somewhat apologetic to his readers. He then proceeds to give a short account, with examples, of the kennings of skaldic poetry, though he does not call them that. He acknowledges in a note that he takes these examples from the work of Paul-Henri Mallet, whose French text he translates quite closely at this point, though with certain omissions, such as references to the giant Ymir, from whose butchered body the gods made the physical world, which he may have thought too outlandish for his readers: 'Il y avoit pour chaque idée une expression poétique, fondée le plus souvent sur quelqu'une des fables de la Mythologie Islandoise, quelquefois aussi sur des rapports naturels. Un Poéte, par exemple, n'osoit guères désigner le ciel, qu'en le nommant *le Crane du Geant Ymer*; L'arc-en-Ciel étoit le *Pont des Dieux*. L'or, *les larmes de Freya*, la poésie le *présent, le breuvage d Odin*. La Terre étoit indifféremment, *l Epouse d Odin, la chair d Ymer*, la *fille de la nuit, le Vaisseau qui flotte sur les âges, la baze des airs*. Les Herbes & les Plantes étoient *sa chevelure, ou sa toison*. Un combat étoit appellé, un *bain de sang, la grêle d Odin, le choc des boucliers*, la mer, *le champ des Pirates, & la ceinture de la terre*. La glace étoit *le plus grand des Ponts*, un vaisseau le cheval des flots; la langue *l épée des paroles* &c' (1755, V, 245-6).

2. In a passage immediately preceding the one quoted above, Mallet makes the following statement: 'Les Grecs, les Romains, & les peuples modernes n'ont eu que des prosateurs en comparaison d'eux; Ils s'étoient fait un langage particulier, dont on ne se servoit jamais que pour les vers, on l'appelloit, come ailleurs, le langage des *Ases*, c'est à dire, des *Dieux*.' I do not know where Percy derived the form *Asom-maal*, which is incorrect, having a dative plural *ásum* instead of a genitive plural, *ása*, as its first element.

PREFACE.

bulous *hiſtory of their gods : and others*
on ſome fancied analogy or reſemblance.
Thus if an Islandic poet had occaſion to
mention a rainbow, he called it, The
bridge of thé gods; *if gold,* The tears
of Freya; *if poeſy,* The gift of Odin.
The earth was indifferently termed, Odin's
ſpouſe; the daughter of night, *or* the
veſſel that floats on the ages: *In like*
manner a battle was to be ſtyled, The
bath of blood; The ſtorm of Odin;
or the claſh of bucklers: *the ſea,* The
field of pirates, *or* the girdle of the
earth. *Ice was not inſignificantly named,*
The greateſt of bridges: *a ſhip,* The
horſe of the waves, &c. †

From the following ſpecimens it will
be

1.

† See theſe and more inſtances in a very ele-
gant *French* book lately publiſhed in *Denmark,*
and often quoted in the following pages, intitled
L' in-

1. This note and the passage of the Preface on skaldic diction to which it is attached demonstrates Percy's knowledge of the first edition of Paul-Henri Mallet's influential account of early Scandinavian history, culture and literature, which was published in two volumes in 1755 and 1756. The information from Mallet in *Five Pieces* must have come from the first edition, as Percy did not receive his copy of the second edition of 1763 until after *Five Pieces* had been published (see *A Chronology of Percy's Translations*). It is interesting that this note asserts optimistically that 'a translation of this work is in great forwardness'. The work, *Northern Antiquities*, was not published until 1770, although it was probably ready for publication several years earlier. Percy had already begun his translation, it would seem, before the publication of Mallet's second edition, something that is borne out by an inspection of his copies of the two editions in the library of The Queen's University, Belfast, the volumes of the first showing many more pencil annotations than the second, which has very few. My guess is that Percy may have continued to use the first edition as his base text even after he had acquired the second.

PREFACE.

be found, that the poetry of the Scalds chiefly displays itself in images of terror. Death and war were their favourite subjects, and in expressions on this head their language is amazingly copious and fruitful. If in the following versions there should be found too frequent a recurrence of synonymous phrases, it is entirely owing to the deficiency of our language, which did not afford a greater variety: for in the original the same thought is scarcely ever expressed twice in the same words. But tho' most of the Islandic poetry, that has been printed, is of the rougher cast; we are not to suppose that the northern bards never addressed themselves to the softer

L' *introduction a l' histoire de Dannemarc par le* Chev. Mallet, 4to. Which contains a most curious and entertaining account of the ancient manners, customs, religion and mythology of the northern nations; besides many striking specimens of their composition. A translation of this work is in great forwardness, and will speedily be published.

passions,

PREFACE.

paffions, or that they did not leave behind them many pieces on the gentler fubjects of love or friendfhip.   The misfortune has been, that their compofitions have fallen into the hands of none but profeffed anti-quarians: and thefe have only felected fuch poems for publication as confirmed

1. *fome fact in hiftory, or ferved to throw light on the antiquities of their country.*

2. *The Editor was in fome doubt whe-ther he fhould fubjoin or fupprefs the originals.   But as they lie within little compafs, and as the books whence they are extracted are very fcarce, he was tempted to add them as vouchers for the authenticity of his verfion.   They have alfo a further ufe.—It has been faid by fome critics * that the prevalence of rhyme in European poetry was de-*

* CRESCEMBENI, &c.

rived

1. Here Percy proclaims himself the promoter of a new approach to ancient poetry, one that differentiated itself from that of 'professed antiquarians' who used poetry as mere source material for historical purposes, by focussing upon the poetry alone as a witness to the nature of the primitive human mind. He enlarged on this approach in a letter of October 1761 to his Welsh correspondent Evan Evans (quoted in Clunies Ross 1998, 45). There he presented the prose context in which much medieval Norse poetry has been transmitted as boring and probably unreliable. The poetry, however, was in his view important as a 'display of ancient manners' and something immediately appealing to a modern readership on account of its 'forcible Images'. Hugh Blair put forward a similar view in *A Critical Dissertation on the Poems of Ossian.*

2. William Shenstone had been adamant that the 'originals', that is, the editions of Old Icelandic texts that Percy worked from (not 'originals' in a modern sense), should be suppressed (see Introduction for a discussion), but by the time *Five Pieces* was published - and the Preface was probably written last - Shenstone was dead. Thus Percy was emboldened to include them and justify their inclusion with several scholarly arguments.

PREFACE.

rived from the Latin hymns, invented
by the monks in the fourth and fifth centuries: but from the original of EGILL's
ODE, it will be feen that the ancient
Gothic poets occafionally ufed rhime with
all the variety and exactnefs of our nicest
moderns, long before their converfion to
chriftianity; and therefore were not likely
to adopt it from the monks; a race of
men, whom they were either unacquainted
with, or held in derifion †.

Upon the whole, it is hoped that the
few pages affigned to the Islandic originals
will not be thought an ufelefs incum-
brance by any readers; but it is prefumed
will be peculiarly acceptable to fuch curious perfons, as ftudy the ancient languages of the north. To thefe gentle-
men this fmall publication is infcribed:

† *Vide infra pag.* 32.

I

One

1. There had been an extensive and complex debate about the origin of rhyme
   in European poetry, going back to the sixteenth century (see Quinn and
   Clunies Ross 1994, 195-204). Some writers defended it as an ornament of
   poetry, others deplored it and urged a return to the quantitative metres of
   classical verse. Many asserted, on the basis of no evidence, that rhyme
   came from the Germanic peoples and particularly the Scandinavians, 'I
   grant that from some Mossie, Idol Oak / In Double Rhymes our Thor and
   Woden spoke' (Lord Roscommon, *Essay on Translated Verse* (1684)).
   Here Percy thinks he has found the evidence that others could not produce,
   Egill's *Hǫfuðlausn*, composed in the verse-form *runhent*, which, unlike
   all other skaldic measures, employs end rhyme (rather than internal rhyme).
   It is of interest that MS Percy c. 7 contains a scribbled note at the bottom
   of f. 28v to the effect that 'The Lines within will prove that the Runic
   Poets used Rhyme, with all the exactness of the modern English Poets.'
   Percy also has a long footnote to the same effect in *Northern Antiquities* I,
   399 and another, in the context of a discussion of Middle English alliterative
   poetry, in *Reliques* II, 260. Ironically, in view of his expressed scorn for
   the hypothesis that rhyme came into European vernacular poetry from the
   Christian Church, and specifically from Latin hymns, which modern
   theorists regard as its most likely origin, scholars of Old Norse versification
   now regard some skaldic verse-forms, certainly *hrynhent* and possibly
   runhent, as inspired at least in part by Latin metres and rhyming practices
   (cf. Faulkes 1999 for a discussion of these verse-forms).

PREFACE.

One of the moſt learned and moſt eminent among them has honoured it ſo far as to compare the verſions every where with the originals. But this was a ſmall exertion of that extenſive ſkill in languages, which the public has ſeen diſplayed with ſo much advantage in the fine editions of JUNIUS'S ETYMOLOGICON *and the* GOTHIC GOSPELS—*That the ſtudy of ancient northern literature hath its important uſes has been often evinced by able writers * : and that it is not dry or unamuſive this little work it is hoped will demonſtrate. Its aim at leaſt is to ſhew, that if thoſe kind of ſtudies are not always employed on works of taſte or claſſic elegance, they ſerve at leaſt to unlock the treaſures of native genius ; they preſent us with frequent ſallies of bold imagi-*

---

* See Dr. Hickes's *Diſſertatio Epiſtolaris, &c.*

nation.

1. The reference is to Percy's neighbour and friend, the Reverend Edward Lye (1694-1767), rector of Yardley Hastings, Northamptonshire and editor of an etymological dictionary of the English language and of the Codex Argenteus of the Gothic Gospels. On Lye, his publications and evidence for the assistance he gave Percy, see Introduction and Clunies Ross 1999.

2. George Hickes's *Dissertatio Epistolaris* forms part of his *Thesaurus* and was composed between 1699 and 1702 (Harris 1992, 58-9 and 80-1). Its aim is to show, by a judicious assembly of mainly Anglo-Saxon but some Norse texts of an historical, political and legal kind, including wills and charters, how the study of 'northern antiquities' could illuminate topical contemporary issues, such as the origin of the jury system and the nature of the English coinage, as well as give an account of early history, law and politics in England and Scandinavia. It is a remarkable work of scholarship, wide-ranging in scope and suggestive, in embryonic form, of much modern research on these subjects.

PREFACE.

nation, and conſtantly afford matter for philoſophical reflection by ſhowing the workings of the human mind in its almoſt original ſtate of nature.

ERRATA.

Page 89. col. 1. line 20. lege
    Fyrer Inndyris eium.

Page 94. col. 1. line 32. lege
    Joſur ſueigde r.

THE

(I.)

THE

INCANTATION

OF

HERVOR.

B

As the attribution on p. 85 prefacing 'the Islandic original' to *The Incantation of Hervor* makes clear, Percy's source for the text of this group of stanzas in the eddic verse-form *fornyrðislag*, usually now referred to in English as *The Waking of Angantýr*, was Olaus Verelius's edition of *Hervarar saga ok Heiðreks konungs*, published at Uppsala in 1672. An entry in Bodleian MS Percy c. 9, f. 99r indicates that he borrowed it from Edward Lye and returned it to him on 30 April 1762. Verelius's was the first printed text of *Hervarar saga* and comprised a parallel text Icelandic-Swedish edition, with Latin notes and glossary, based on a mid-seventeeth century paper manuscript of dubious reliability, Uppsala University Library R 715. As it is doubtful whether Percy could read either Swedish or Icelandic sufficiently well to benefit a great deal from the edition, his citation of it in *Five Pieces* may owe a good deal to Edward Lye's encouragement and the Latin notes and glossary. However, he knew other sources for both the Icelandic text and an English translation of this already popular Norse poem. His notebook Bodleian MS Percy c. 7, where various drafts and notes relating to *The Incantation of Hervor* are to be found, shows on ff. 29r-v and 33v that he was also familiar with passages from *Hervarar saga* quoted and discussed in Bartholin 1689, which he used as a source for a few of his notes.

As he indicates in his Introduction to the poem (p. 4), Percy's English translation comes from George Hickes's version in his *Thesaurus* I, 193-5, 'with some considerable emendations'. Hickes also used Verelius's edition as the basis of his Icelandic text, though he makes some changes to it, particularly in the layout of the verses and the omission of linking prose passages. There are also a few errors in the transcription of the Icelandic. Although it is not mentioned in the *Thesaurus*, the English translation was not Hickes's own work, but probably that of a Swedish diplomat resident at the time in London, Christopher Leyencrona, or another Swede of his acquaintance (for the evidence, see Harris 1992, 268, letter 99, Chamberlayne to Wanley, 7 January 1699). The English translation, as might be expected, follows the Swedish translation rather more closely in some respects than it does the Icelandic text (see Fell 1996 for an analysis). Hickes's publication identified this group of stanzas as a poem in its own right, outside the context of the saga in which they, and other verses, have been preserved. He did so in the scholarly context of a comparison between Old English diction and verse-forms and Old Norse *fornyrðislag*, used for poetry in eddic measures, as these stanzas are. The effect was to allow the verses, identified as an independent poem, to be appreciated separately from the saga, something Percy drew attention to in his Preface as distinguishing his own approach from that of 'professed antiquarians'.

The English translation in the *Thesaurus* was also printed in *Dryden's Miscellany* 6, 387 (1716), as Percy notes in Percy c. 7, f. 3r. Other publications derived from the translation in Hickes were in the *Lady's Magazine* for June 1761, 487-9 and the *Annual Register* 4 (1761), 236-7. In the later part of the eighteenth century numerous versions of the poem, many still loosely based on Hickes, testify to its popularity (see Collins, Table III to Clunies Ross 1998, 248-253 for the details). I have suggested (Clunies Ross 1998, 26 and note 7) that the identification of female readers with the figure of Hervǫr may have played some part in the poem's growing popularity. However, even without its heroine, *The Incantation of Hervor* provided a winning recipe of sublime elements to capture the imagination of those with a taste for 'ancient' poetry, including the raising of the dead from grave-mounds surrounded by flames, a fateful ancestral sword, Tyrfingr, and a dramatic dialogue between a dead hero, Angantýr, and his only daughter, Hervǫr, keen to play a son's part and inherit the weapon.

Modern scholars who have discussed the Hickes and Percy versions of *The Waking of Angantýr* are Bennett 1938, Dickins 1962 and Fell 1996. 'The Incantation of Hervor' is Smith 1989, PeT 21, 42 and 43 and Clunies Ross 1998, 1, p. 86.

The following page, B1b, is blank.

INTRODUCTION.

" A NDGRYM the grandfather
"   of Hervor, was prince of a
" part of Sweden, now in the province
" of Smaland: He forcibly carried away
" out of Ruffia Eyvor the daughter of
" Suafurlama, by whom he had twelve
" fons, four whereof were Hervardur,
" Hiorvardur, Hrani, and Angantyr the
" father of Hervor. Thefe twelve bre-
" thren, according to the ufual practice
" of thofe times, followed piracy. In
" one of their expeditions they landed
" in the territories of Hialmar king of
" Thulemark, where a fierce battle en-
" fuing they all loft their lives. An-
" gantyr fell the laft of his brethren,
" having firft with his own hand killed
" their adverfary Hialmar. They were

                    B 2   " buried

A draft version of the Introductory paragraph, headed 'Advertisment', is on f.3v of Bodleian MS Percy c. 7 and some further notes towards it, copied from Verelius, are on f. 33v.

[4]

" buried in the field of battle, together
" with their arms : and it is at their
" tombs that Hervor, the daughter of
" Angantyr, who had taken a voyage
" thither on purpofe, makes the follow-
" ing invocation."

" N. B. This Piece is publifhed from
" the tranflation of Dr. Hickes, with
" fome confiderable emendations ; See
" his *Thefaurus Antiq. Literaturæ Sep-*
" *tentrion. Tom. 1. p. 193.*

1.   " The *Hervarer Saga*, whence this
" poem is extracted, is an old Islandic
" hiftory *, the author and date of
" which are unknown : but it is be-
" lieved, in general, to be of very great

2.   * *Saga* in the Iflandic language fignifies a
HISTORY, &c.

                                        " anti-

1. This paragraph, plus some additional unpublished material, exists in draft in Bodleian MS Percy c. 7, f. 3r. As usual, Percy is at pains to point out the 'very great antiquity' of his source text. Modern scholarship usually places the composition of *Hervarar saga* at c. 1250, but much of the poetry it contains is likely to be considerably older. Aside from *The Waking of Angantýr*, other verses in this saga that are generally now treated as independent poems are *Hlǫðskviða*, or *The Battle of the Goths and the Huns*, and *Heiðreks gátur*, or *The Riddles of Heiðrekr and Gestumblindi*.

2. It is probable that the word 'saga' would have been unknown to many of Percy's readers. Its first recorded use in English (*OED*, *saga* [1], sense 1 a) is by George Hickes (1709), whose wording is very close to Percy's here and may have been his source: 'The histories of the old Northern nations, which commonly have the title of Saga, which signifies a narration of History' (Hickes in *Pepys Diary* (1879) VI. 201). The Old Icelandic noun *saga* f., covers quite a wide semantic field, including the following senses: 'that which is said, statement, report, story, narrative, history'.

[5]

" antiquity. It records the atchieve-
" ments of Hervor, a celebrated nor-
" thern heroine, as alfo the exploits of
" her anceftors and defcendants, in Swe-
" den and other northern countries. It
" was printed in a thin folio vol. at
" Upfal in 1672, with a Swedifh ver-
" fion and Latin notes by Olaus Vere-
" lius : and contains many other pieces
" of Runic poetry."

[6]

1.

" *To prevent as much as possible the*
" *interruption of notes, it was thought*
" *proper to premise a few miscellaneous*
" *observations.*

I.

2.

" THE northern nations held their
" Runic verses in such reverence,
" that they believed them sufficient (pro-
" vided they were pronounced with great
" emotion of mind) to raise the ghosts
" of the departed : and that without
" other magical rites, especially if the
" the party had worked himself up in-
" to

1. In Percy's notebook, Bodleian MS Percy c. 7, ff. 3v-4v, these 'miscellaneous observations' bear the heading 'Notes' (f.4r). Doubtless, he was following Shenstone's advice in collecting as many notes into the form of a preface as he could.

2. Section I of the 'miscellaneous observations' is mainly derived from Verelius's notes on pp. 97-100 of his edition, though with a greater stress at the beginning on the reverential status of 'Runic verses' in ancient Scandinavia. Cf. Thomas Gray's representation of Óðinn as using a 'runic rhyme' to raise the seeress in his version of *Baldrs Draumar*, *The Descent of Odin*. The fact that Verelius usually translates Norse verses he quotes in the notes into Latin was very helpful to Percy.

[7]

" to a firm perfuasion that it would hap-
" pen according to his defires. ———
" Hervor therefore in the firft ftanza
" or ftrophe calls upon her father to
" awake and deliver to her his fword.
" —— This not fucceeding, in the next
" place fhe adjures him and his bre-
" thren by all their arms, THE SHIELD,
" &c. ——— Being ftill unanfwered,
" fhe wonders that her father and un-
" cles fhould be fo mouldered to duft,
" as that nothing of them fhould re-
" main, and adds, as it were by way of
" imprecation, SO MAY YOU ALL
" BE, &c. a form of conjuring not pe-
" culiar to this poem, Olaus Verelius
" quotes a like paffage from another
" ancient piece to the following effect.

Alla quelie eitur ver
Innan rifia, oc vefta bal :

B 4   *Nema*

[8]

Nema fuerdid felier mier
Samit rauda jotna mal.

" May the poifon of ferpents and
noxious flames torment you all within
your ribs, unlefs you deliver me the
fword adorned with gold."

Vid. Herv. Saga, pag. 100, *&c.*

1.

II.

" By *Duergar* or DWARFS, the an-
" cient Scandinavians did not under-
" ftand human creatures defective in fize
" or ftature, but a diftinct race of
" beings, a kind of leffer demons,
" who inhabited the rocks and moun-
" tains, and were remarkably expert at
" forging weapons, that were proof
" againft all force or fraud.———They
" meant

1. The draft text for Section II is on f. 7v of Percy c. 7, and includes a comparison between the dwarves of 'the ancient Celtic Mythology' [*sic*] and the classical Cyclops, which Percy has omitted in his published text. It derives from a footnote to Hickes's version of the poem (*Thesaurus* I, 194, note 1). A different version of his text on dwarves, which includes a reference to Verelius as here, is on f. 33v. There Percy describes dwarves as 'a kind of half dæmons, inhabitants of the Mountains, who forged arms, which were proof against all force or fraud', concluding with an additional reference, 'sed Vid. Edd. Myth. 13'. This is a reference to Peder Resen's edition of Snorri Sturluson's *Edda*, which his friend Lye also owned. On a different leaf of the ms, f. 25r, Percy has copied a list of dwarves' names, which is similar to, but not the same as that in Resen's text of the *Gylfaginning* section of the *Edda* (1665, ed. Faulkes 1977, *Mythologia XII, De Nanis*), without any comment. He probably found the reference in Hickes *Thesaurus* I, p. 193, note 3. The inclusion of these passages in his notebook suggests that the subject of the dwarves of Old Norse myth had a special interest for him, as indeed it had for Hickes. The word 'dwarf' had existed in the English language since Anglo-Saxon times, in the sense of a human being much below normal size and stature (*OED*, *dwarf*, sb., sense A 1 a), but its Norse sense of a mythological figure with special skills in metal working was new, the *OED*'s first recorded use in this sense (A 1 b) being from Percy's own *Northern Antiquities*.

[9]

" meant by *dwarfs*, much the fame as
" we do by *fairies*."

Olaus Ver. ad Her. Sag. p. 44. 45.
Hickes Thef. tom. 2. p. 311.

1.

III.

" As to what is faid in the fecond ftan-
" za, of their being buried UNDER THE
" ROOTS OF TREES. It may be ob-
" ferved, that the northern nations, in
" the firft ages, ufually burnt their
" dead: afterwards they buried them
" under a *barrow* or hillock of earth,
" &c. but no author mentions the roots
" of trees, as chofen particularly for the
" place of interment. There is, indeed,
" one inftance of this to be found, in a
" fragment of an ancient Runic poem
" preferved in the hiftory of Snorro
                                " Sturlefon,

1. Section III corresponds to f. 4v of Bodleian MS Percy c. 7. Percy's source here is Johan Peringskiöld's 1697 edition of the Icelander Snorri Sturluson's *Heimskringla* of c. 1230 (see further *Percy's translations of Old Norse poetry in Bodleian MS Percy c. 7, 1. Translations from the works of Viking Age skalds*). The information about the ages of burning and burial in a mound comes from Snorri's Preface to this work, while the 'fragment of an ancient Runic poem' quoted here is stanzas 6 and 7 of Eyvindr skáldaspillir's *Háleygjatal*, which Percy came upon in Peringskiöld (they are in ch. 23 of *Ynglinga saga*). See *Translations from the works of Viking Age skalds*, 1.2 for a different version of these stanzas, which Percy had had rejected by Shenstone. He sneaked them in here as 'miscellaneous observations' to *The Incantation of Hervor*.

[10]

" Sturlefon, but it feems to be attended
" with circumftances too particular to
" prove the generality of the practice."

———*Bith ofur capp,*
Auftur konga &c.

" —The eaftern kings contended together with vehement rage, when the
fons of Yngvon hanged the generous
king on a tree.

" And there on a promontory is that
ancient tree, on which the dead body
was fufpended : where the promontory
Straumyernes divides the bay ; there,
I fay, expofed to the winds, ftands that
moft noted tree, remarkable for the
tomb and monument * of the king."

Snorro Sturl. Hift. Reg. Sept. fol. p. 28.

1.

* Or rather *barrow,* Lat. *tumulus.*

IV.

1. Percy follows the Latin translation in Peringskiöld here (1697, 28), which has 'Ibi, inquam, notissima illa arbor ventis exposita, *tumulo regio & cippo insignis est* ' [my italics]. The Icelandic equivalent to the italicised phrase is, in Peringskiöld's version, 'Um fylkis hrör/ Steine merktur'. The note serves no scholarly purpose but simply draws attention to the 'gothic' detail of the reference to the grave mound.

[11]

IV.

" THE northern nations believed that
" the tombs of their heroes emitted a
" kind of lambent flame, which was
" always vifible in the night, and ferv-
" ed to guard the afhes of the dead.
" They called it *Hauga Elldr,* or THE
" SEPULCHRAL FIRE. It was fuppofed
" more particularly to furround fuch
" tombs as contained hidden treafures."
Barthol. de contempt. a Dan. Mort. p. 275.

V.

" MOST of the proper names in the
" ancient northern languages were
" fignificant. Thus *Angantyr* fignifies
" One who bravely does his duty." *Her-*
vardur, " A preferver of the army." *Hior-*
vardur, " A keeper of the fword." *&c.*
Vid. Ol. Verel. ad Herv. Saga, p. 49.

5

1. The passage of Bartholin (1689, 275) from which Percy derives this note is not copied into his Bodleian notebook. Bartholin's text at this point refers to *Hervarar saga* as an example of early Scandinavian beliefs in the fire associated with grave mounds: 'Vocabatur is ignis *Hauga elldr* seu *ignis tumularum*, & noctu conspectus, thesaurum in tumulo contentum prodere crcditus.'
2. Notes from Verelius towards this Section are on f. 33v of Percy c. 7.

    The following page, B6b, is blank.

THE

INCANTATION

O F

HERVOR.

AWAKE, Angantyr; Hervor,
the only daughter of thee and
Suafu, doth awaken thee. Give me,
out of the tomb, the hardened fword,
which the dwarfs made for Suafurlama.

Hervardur, Hiorvardur, Hrani, and
Angantyr; with helmet and coat of
mail, and a fharp fword; with fhield
and accoutrements and bloody fpear, I
wake you all under the roots of trees.

ARE

As Percy states, he is following the English translation in Hickes's *Thesaurus* but, he claims, 'with some considerable emendations'. These 'emendations' are recorded in the following notes, and it can be seen that there are very few instances where they are 'considerable'. There are no differences between Hickes and Percy in the first two verses, excluding minor variations of punctuation and spelling. Neither knows enough Icelandic grammar to give the correct nominative forms of Sváfa and Sváfrlami, even though, in his notebook, Percy records 'Egvor was the daughter of Suafurlama (lami Lat.)' (f.33v) and the Swedish translation in Verelius pointed the way with 'Och modrens Swafas' and 'Swafurlame'. Evidently the Hicksian influence was too strong. Fell 1996, 51 makes a claim that the Swedish translator whom Hickes engaged, rather than Hickes himself, is likely to have been responsible for these errors, but it is hard to see why he would have been if he was working from the Swedish text in Verelius.

[14]

ARE the fons of Andgrym, who delighted in mifchief, now become duft and afhes? Can none of Eyvor's fons now fpeak with me out of the habitations of the dead? Hervardur, Hiorvardur!

So may you all be, within your ribs, as a thing that is hanged up to putrefy among infects, unlefs you deliver me the fword, which the dwarfs made, * * * and the glorious belt.

[HERE the tomb opens, the infide of which appears all on fire, and the following words are fung out of the tomb.]

ANGANTYR.
DAUGHTER Hervor, full of fpells to raife the dead, why doeft thou call fo?
Wilt

1.

1. To this point Percy follows Hickes, the only significant change being a more accurate spelling of 'Hervardur' beside Hickes's 'Harvardur'. Both they and Verelius have a defective text for the fourth stanza, and consequently find it difficult to extract much meaning from it. The problems are compounded by Verelius's confessed inability to understand 'i maura/ Mornid hangi' (modern editors preferring 'í maura/ morniÐ haugi', '[as if] you mouldered away in an ant-hill'). Hickes, in a lengthy and impressive note, actually got the correct meaning for *maurr*, translating 'insects', as he says 'Maur, formica; species metonymice pro genere' (I, 193, note 4). Percy noted this on f. 4r of Percy c. 7 but refrains from mentioning it in print.

   The prose passage that follows this verse is not in Hickes. Percy must have translated it out of Verelius (though not very closely), perhaps with Lye's help (there is a Latin summary on p. 97 of Verelius's notes).

[15]

Wilt thou run on to thy own mifchief?
Thou art mad and out of thy fenfes,
who art defperately refolved to waken
1. dead men.

I was not buried either by father or
other friends : two which lived after
me got Tirfing; one of whom is now
poffeffor thereof *,

HERVOR.

Thou doft not tell the truth.   So let
Odin preferve thee fafe in the tomb, as
thou haft not Tirfing by thee.   Art thou
unwilling, Angantyr, to give an inheri-
2. tance to thy only child ?

AN-

* This is faid merely to make her defift from
her purpofe ; as forefeeing it will prove fatal to her
pofterity.
Tirfing is the name of the fword.   The etymology of this word is not known.

1. Verelius has a lengthy note on pp.97-8 on this stanza, with a Latin translation of the whole verse and an explanation of the Icelandic phrase *full feiknstafa*, 'full of malicious staves' [presumably runic staves] or, as he writes, 'caracteribus magicis plena'. There is no difference between Hickes's and Percy's translations either of this verse or the next, except for Percy's note, which is not in Hickes. The draft note is on f. 5v of Percy c. 7.

2. This is the first example of a 'considerable emendation' to Hickes's English translation. Percy has corrected Hickes's 'so let Odin hide thee in the tombe, as thu hast Tirfing by thee' by changing 'hide' to 'preserve thee safe' ('so lati As þig/ Heilan i haugi' in Verelius) and making the following clause negative, 'as thou hast not Tirfing by thee' ('Sem þu hafir eigi/ Tirfing med þier' in Verelius). Both these changes correct errors in Hickes's translation.

[16]

ANGANTYR.

I will tell thee, Hervor, what will come to pafs : this Tirfing will, if thou doft believe me, deftroy almoft all thy offspring. Thou fhalt have a fon, who afterwards muft poffefs Tirfing, and many think he will be called Heidrek by the people.

HERVOR.

I do by inchantments make that the dead fhall never enjoy reft, unlefs Angantyr deliver me Tirfing; that cleaveth fhields, and killed Hialmar.

ANGANTYR.

YOUNG maid, I fay, thou art of manlike courage, who doft rove about by night to tombs, with fpear engraven
with

1. Hickes's translation has a row of asterisks at the end of this verse, but Percy has supplied the translation 'that cleaveth shields, and killed Hialmar' for Verelius's 'Hlyfum hættan,/ Hialmars bana', 'dangerous to shields, the killer of Hjálmar' [of Tyrfingr]. Hickes's asterisks are rather puzzling, for the Swedish translation in Verelius ('Som klyfwer sköllder/ Och dråpte Hialmar') should have been easy to follow for his presumed Swedish assistant.

[17]

with magic fpells *, with helmet and
coat of mail, before the door of our
hall.

HERVOR.

I took thee for a brave man, before I
found out your hall. Give me, out of the
tomb, the workmanfhip of the dwarfs,
which hateth all coats of mail. It is
not good for thee to hide it.

ANGANTYR.

The death of Hialmar lies under my
fhoulders : it is all wrapt up in fire : I
know no maid, in any country, that
dares take this fword in hand.

1.
* It was ufual with the northern warriors to in-
fcribe Runic characters on their weapons, to prevent their being dulled or blunted by inchantment,
as alfo to give them a keennefs and ftrength which
nothing could refift. *Ol. Verel. pag.* 101.

C   HERVOR.

1. A draft of this note is on f. 6v of MS Percy c. 7, in which 'magic characters' appears instead of 'Runic characters' and 'evil Arts' appears instead of 'inchantment'. These changes reflect the emphasis of Percy's first 'miscellaneous observation' to this poem on pp. 6 and 7 that Runic verses alone without 'other magical rites' were thought sufficient by early Northern nations to perform supernatural feats, and suggest an unwillingness on his part to connect 'Runic poetry' with sorcery and black magic.

[18]

HERVOR.

I fhall keep and take in my hand the fharp fword, if I may obtain it. I do not think that fire will burn, which plays about the fight of deceafed men.

ANGANTYR.

O conceited Hervor, thou art mad: rather than thou, in a moment, fhouldeft fall into the fire, I will give thee the fword out of the tomb, young maid; and not hide it from thee.

1. [Here the fword was delivered to Hervor out of the tomb, who proceeds thus.]

HERVOR.

Thou didft well, thou offspring of heroes, that thou didft fend me the fword

out

1. This prose passage is in Verelius but is omitted by Hickes. It runs 'Þa var suerd i hendi Hervarar, oc quad hon:', 'Med thet samma fick hon swerdet i hand/ och qwad:'.

[19]

out of the tomb; I am now better pleafed,
O prince, to have it, than if I had
gotten all Norway.

Angantyr.

Falfe woman, thou doft not un-
derftand that thou fpeakeft foolifhly of
that in which thou doeft rejoice: for
Tirfing fhall, if thou doeft believe me,
maid, deftroy all thy offspring.

Hervor.

I muft go to my feamen. Here I
have no mind to ftay longer. Little do
I care, O royal anceftor, about what
my fons may hereafter quarrel.

Angantyr.

Take and keep Hialmar's bane,
which thou fhalt long have and enjoy :

1. Percy's text differs from Hickes's here, the latter reading' Little do I care, O Royall freind, what my sons hereafter quarrell about'. The change from 'freind' in the sense of kinsman to 'ancestor' relates to the Icelandic 'Lofdunga vinur', 'friend of princes', that is, one who consorts with princes, in this case, Angantýr. Percy's alteration does not really bring the translation closer to the sense of the Icelandic.

[20]

touch but the edges of it, there is
poifon in them both: it is a moft cruel
devourer of men.

HERVOR.

I fhall keep, and take in hand, the
fharp fword, which thou haft let me
have: I do not fear, O flain father,
about what my fons may hereafter
quarrel.

ANGANTYR.

Farewel, daughter: I do quickly
give thee twelve men's death : if thou
canft believe with might and courage :
even all the goods, which Andgrym's
fons left behind them.

HERVOR.

Dwell all of you fafe in the tomb.
I muft be gone, and haften hence ; for
I feem to be in the midft of a place
where fire burneth round about me.

THE

Although Percy's text does not deviate from Hickes's in any significant respect in these final verses, their English text is frequently relatively far from the Icelandic in Verelius, corrupt as it often is. Even Verelius's Latin notes are not used. The Swedish translation is mostly followed here, though changes occur in the English that are not found there either, for example, the use of the present tense in the last verse's 'for I seem to be in the midst of a place where fire burneth round about me' for the preterite of both the Icelandic and the Swedish.

(II.)

T H E

D Y I N G   O D E

O F

REGNER LODBROG.

C 3

This late twelfth-century poem, whose name is now known among scholars of Old Icelandic as *Krákumál*, 'Lay of Kráka' (='Crow', the nickname of Ragnarr's second wife Áslaug), achieved a paradigmatic status in the eighteenth century as that Viking poem which most memorably expressed the key themes that were then thought to dominate Old Norse poetry: war, ferocity, and stoical fortitude in the face of death, all expressed in strong, terror-inspiring images by means of a monologue placed in the mouth of the archetypal Viking hero Ragnarr loðbrók ('hairy breeches'), as he lay dying in the snake-pit that his adversary, King Ælla of Northumbria, had prepared for his torture and destruction. In this monologue Ragnarr reviews each of the fifty-one battles he has fought during his life and concludes with a stanza in which he looks forward to death in the expectation of being transported to Valhalla by Óðinn's valkyries.

Krákumál, although an independent poem, is associated in some medieval manuscripts with the Icelandic prose saga *Ragnars saga loðbrókar*, which tells the stories of Ragnarr, his wives and his sons, who were almost as famous as he was in heroic legend. The poem first became known to the European literary world through the runic version, with interlinear Latin glosses and Latin notes, that appeared in the appendix to Ole Worm's *Literatura Runica* of 1636, 197-227. Percy claims to print Worm's text of the 'Islandic original' (see pp. 88-92), but he makes no attempt to reproduce the runes there (though a few snatches appear on the title page to *Five Pieces*), and probably owes a good deal to the version of the poem's text in Bartholin (see below). Worm's version of the poem became known to English scholars in the seventeenth century, and parts of it were quoted and explained by Robert Sheringham, *De Anglorum Gentis Origine Disceptatio* (1670) and Aylett Sammes, *Britannica Antiqua Illustrata* (1676). Sir William Temple ('Of Heroick Virtue', in *Miscellanea* 1692) uses both Worm and Sheringham in his discussion of Ragnarr, and several eighteenth-century writers followed suit (for details of the English reception of this poem, see Collins in Clunies Ross 1998, 248-253 and Appendix 2). When Percy brought out his translation in *Five Pieces*, this poem was probably better known to his readers than any others of the selection, though none of the earlier versions were complete. Translations were also available in other European languages: in Dutch, by Lambert ten Kate (1723), in Swedish, by Erik Julius Björner (1737) and in French, by Paul-Henri Mallet (1756), the latter version being in part Percy's inspiration for his English translation. Later, a Danish version by B. C. Sandvig followed in 1779 and a German one by Friedrich David Gräter in 1789 (see further Heinrichs 1993).

As the title page to *Five Pieces* makes clear, 'The Dying Ode of Regner

Lodbrog' achieved its fame in the eighteenth century partly through several appropriately barbaric and sublime images that were frequently quoted by writers on northern antiquities. Two of them are cited in Worm's runic version on the title page: the image of Viking heroes drinking beer from the skulls of their enemies, and the image of the hero who dies laughing. The third was, in the words of Percy's translation, 'The pleasure of that day [when Ragnarr and his men fought in Northumbria] was like kissing a young widow at the highest seat of the table' (p.34). This passage seemed to offer an interesting equation between the conduct of war and sexual adventure. However, both this and the first image were based on misunderstandings of the Norse text, and it took a long time for these persuasive mistakes to be exposed and corrected (Clunies Ross 1998, 232 and see notes to Percy's translation below).

Percy used both Ole Worm's text and the extensive quotation and commentary on this poem that he found in Bartholin 1689, for whom it was a key example of the ancient Scandinavians' defiance of death. Percy's Bodleian manuscript notebook contains transcriptions of Bartholin's version of the poem (1689, 42, 318, 424, 428, 515, 524, 525, 531, 541, 557, 558 and 608) copied out on small scraps of paper, often the backs of address pages from letters. These transcripts are on ff. 12r-v, 13-19 (recto sides only), 20r-v and 21-23 (recto sides only). They must have been of great assistance to Percy in decoding Worm's runic text for 'the Islandic original', but he could have made better use than he did of the generally more accurate Latin translation in Bartholin. Percy also had assistance from Edward Lye; there are several pages of Lye's glosses, some relating to this poem, on ff. 36r -39r of Percy c. 7. Worm's text, which was produced by the Icelander Magnús Olafsson, is closely related to a manuscript in Uppsala University Library, R 702. In Smith 1989, 'The Dying Ode of Regner Lodbrog' is PeT 17 and 21 and it is Clunies Ross 1998, 2, p. 86. The verse-form of the poem is *háttlausa*, a variant of the skaldic measure *dróttkvætt* without internal rhyme.

The following page, C3b, is blank.

[23]

INTRODUCTION.

" **K**ING Regner Lodbrog was a
" celebrated Poet, Warrior, and
" (what was the fame thing in thofe
" ages) Pirate; who reigned in Denmark,
" about the beginning of the ninth cen-
" tury. After many warlike expeditions
" by fea and land, he at length met with
" bad fortune. He was taken in battle by
" his adverfary Ella king of Northum-
" berland. War in thofe rude ages was
" carried on with the fame inhumani-
" ty, as it is now among the favages of
" North-America : their prifoners were
" only referved to be put to death with
" torture. Regner was accordingly
" thrown into a dungeon to be ftung

C 4   " to

[24]

" to death by ferpents.   While he was
" dying he compofed this fong, where-
" in he records all the valiant atchieve-
" ments of his life, and threatens Ella
" with vengeance; which hiftory in-
" forms us was afterwards executed by
" the fons of Regner.

" It is, after all, conjectured that Reg-
" ner himfelf only compofed a few ftan-
" zas of this poem, and that the reft
" were added by his *Scald* or poet-
" laureat, whofe bufinefs it was to add
" to the folemnities of his funeral by
" finging fome poem in his praife.
        L'Edda par Chev. Mallet. p. 150.

" This piece is tranflated from the
" Islandic original publifhed by Olaus
" Wormius in his *Literatura Runica,*
                    " *Hafniæ*

1. Ívarr, Bjǫrn, Hvítserkr and Sigurðr, the sons of Ragnarr by his second wife Áslaug (Kráka), sought vengeance for their father's death at the hands of King Ælla of Northumbria and their exploits, particularly their attacks in various parts of Anglo-Saxon England, are mentioned in Icelandic sagas (mainly *Ragnars saga loðbrókar* and *Ragnars sona þáttr*), Saxo grammaticus (*Gesta Danorum* Book 9) and a number of Anglo-Saxon historical sources (see Smith 1935 and McTurk 1991). In all probability, these legends' connections with England and English history enhanced the popularity of 'The Dying Ode of Regner Lodbrog' for Percy's British readers, as they could regard it as a part of their own national history.

2. Most of Percy's Introduction to the poem is based on Mallet's introduction to his abridged version in *Monumens de la mythologie et de la poésie des Celtes* (1756, 265-7), with a few additional remarks, including the comparison with 'the savages of North-America', and the precise location of Ælla's kingdom in Northumberland. Mallet's text is drastically abridged and altered to suit his readers' tastes, by removing parts that he considered tedious or obscure. By contrast, Percy's version is much fuller even though it is not without errors. For the most part, his translation follows the Latin interlinear gloss in Worm's edition, and most of the errors originate there.

[25]

1.   " *Hafniæ* 4*to.* 1631.——*Ibidem*, 2. *Edit.*
      " *Fol.* 1651.

" N. B. Thora, mentioned in the
" firſt ſtanza, was daughter of ſome
" little Gothic prince, whoſe palace
" was infeſted by a large ſerpent; he
" offered his daughter in marriage to
" any one that would kill the monſter
" and ſet her free. Regner accom-
" pliſhed the atchievement and acquir-
" ed the name of *Lod-brog*, which ſig-
" nifies ROUGH or HAIRY-BREECHES,
" becauſe he cloathed himſelf all over
" in rough or hairy ſkins before he
" made the attack. [*Vide Saxon Gram.*
2.   " *pag.* 152, 153.]——This is the poe-
                                    " tical

1. The first edition of Worm's *Literatura Runica* was published in 1636 not 1631. Percy gets the date right on p. 88.
2. This reference is to Saxo Grammaticus's *Gesta Danorum*, Book 9, in the Frankfurt 1576 reprint of the first edition by Christian Pedersen, published in Paris in 1514. Percy took this reference from Worm's notes (1636, 198).

[26]

" tical account of this adventure : but
" hiftory informs us that Thora was
" kept prifoner by one of her father's
" vaffals, whofe name was *Orme* or
" SERPENT, and that it was from this
" man that Regner delivered her, clad
" in the aforefaid fhaggy armour. But
" he himfelf chufes to commemorate it
" in the moft poetical manner."

Vide Chev. Mallet Introd. à l' Hift.
de Dannemarc. pag. 201.

THE

Percy's note on the story of Ragnarr and his first wife Þóra is indebted both to the Latin notes to Worm's edition (p.198) and to Mallet 1755, 201-2. Mallet presents Ragnarr's winning of Þóra as 'un exploit de Galanterie', in line with his hypothesis that courtly love and the medieval romance were imported to France and other parts of Southern Europe from Scandinavia. For Mallet, one of the main reasons to present any part of the text of this poem was as evidence in support of this hypothesis. The explanation of the meaning of Ragnarr's by-name *loðbrók* appears to have come from Sheringham 1670, 380, whom Percy quotes in Latin on this topic in Percy c. 7, f. 4v.

[27]

THE

DYING ODE

OF

REGNER LODBROG.

1. WE fought with fwords : * * *
    when in Gothland I flew an
    enormous ferpent : my reward was the
    beauteous Thora. Thence I was deem-
    ed a man : they called me Lodbrog from
    that flaughter. * * * I thruft the monfter
    through with my fpear, with the fteel
    productive of fplendid rewards.

    We fought with fwords : I was very
    young, when towards the Eaft, in the
    ftraights of Eirar, we gained rivers of
                                        blood

1. An analysis of Percy's translation technique in this verse gives a good
    indication of his general method in 'The Dying Ode of Regner Lodbrog'.
    For the most part his translation follows the Latin gloss above the runic
    lines in Worm, but this often gives only a very sketchy guide to the meaning.
    In two places in this stanza Percy completely fails to follow the gloss.
    Line 2 of the Icelandic, *hitt vas æ* [or, *ei*] *fyr lǫngu*, 'it happened [not] a
    long time ago' attracts the Latin gloss *haud post longum tempus...*', 'it
    was not at all after a long time...' which Percy represents by a row of
    asterisks; these, he established in the Preface, indicate that the passage
    was obscure to him, and he may have been in doubt over the meaning of *æ*
    [*ei*], where one could choose the meaning 'not' or 'ever'. 'I slew an
    enormous serpent' is close to the Latin gloss *ad serpentis immensi necem*,
    but does not attempt to incorporate the Latin note's explanation of the
    snake-kenning *grafvitnir*, 'digging wolf [lit. 'being with keen senses']' as
    serpens quia terram fodit. There is a second snake-kenning in line 7, which
    is also explained in a note, but not attempted by Percy (his second row of
    asterisks covers it). In 'my reward was the beauteous Thora', Percy
    embroiders the Latin *tunc impetravimus Thoram*, which follows the
    Icelandic *þá fingum vér Þóru*, 'then we [I] obtained Thora [as my bride]'
    by highlighting the sense of reward and introducing mention of her beauty,
    a detail absent from both Latin and Icelandic. Clearly, Percy is here
    influenced by Mallet's concept of Ragnarr loðbrók as a dashing proto-
    romantic hero, gaining his bride as a reward for his acts of gallantry. There
    is another idea, not present in the Icelandic in so many words (though
    perhaps implicit in the verse sequence) but suggested by a mistranslation
    in the Latin gloss, which assists Mallet and Percy in their idea of Ragnarr
    as a romantic lover or even a figure similar to a folk-tale hero. This is the
    notion that his rescue of Thora was an initiatory, man-making exploit, that
    turned him into the mature hero who could then go out and win many
    battles. Percy's 'thence I was deemed a man', just like the Latin *ex hoc
    vocarunt me virum*, is at odds with the Icelandic text, *þaðan hétu mik
    fyrðar*, where *fyrðar*, 'men' is the subject of the sentence not a direct object,
    'after that [or 'because of that'] men called me ...*loðbrók* [i.e. after the
    battle in which I killed the dragon]. The final line, 'with the steel productive
    of splendid rewards' follows the Latin gloss closely.

[28]

blood * for the ravenous wolf: ample
food for the yellow-footed fowl.   There
the hard iron fung upon the lofty
helmets.   The whole ocean was one
wound.   The raven waded in the blood
of the flain.

We fought with fwords : we lifted
high our lances ; when I had numbered twenty years, and every where acquired great renown.   We conquered
eight barons at the mouth of the Da-
nube.   We procured ample entertain-
ment for the eagle in that flaughter.
Bloody fweat fell in the ocean of wounds.
A hoft of men there loft their lives.

* Literally " Rivers of wounds."——
By the yellow-footed fowl is meant the eagle.

We

1. Percy's 'and everywhere acquired great renown' follows an error in Worm's Latin gloss and notes, where the Icelandic *ok tjǫr ruðum víða*, 'and we reddened swords widely', is misunderstood. He follows Worm's gloss in translating the Icelandic *geri*, 'the greedy one' as 'eagle' rather than 'wolf', the latter perhaps its more common meaning, even though he copied out a passage from Bartholin (1689, 424) on f. 19r of Percy c. 7 which glossed *gera* here as *lupo odini*.

2. Percy is here misled by Worm's Latin gloss (*vulnerum amnes*, 'rivers of wounds') and note to the word *undarm* (*recte undarn*) in line 4, *undarn frekum vargi*, '[we provided] a morning meal for the greedy wolf'. He should have followed the Latin translation in Bartholin, '... cadavera voraci lupo', which he copied into his notebook (Percy c. 7, f. 20r). Worm's gloss and note to line 9's *sollinn*, 'swollen, disturbed' (of the sea) also misleads Percy into 'the whole ocean was one wound', based on *omnis erat oceanus vulnus*. The same mistake occurs in the penultimate line of the following stanza.

[29]

We fought with fwords : we enjoyed
the fight, when we fent the inhabitants
of Helfing to the habitation of the
gods †. We failed up the Viftula.
Then the fword acquired fpoils : the
whole ocean was one wound : the earth
grew red with reeking gore : the fword
grinned at the coats of mail : the fword
1.   cleft the fhields afunder.

We fought with fwords : I well re-
member that no one fled that day in the
battle before in the fhips Herauder fell.
There does not a fairer warrior divide
the ocean with his veffels. * * * This
prince ever brought to the battle a gallant heart.

† Literally, " to the hall of Odin."

                                              We

1. Worm's notes to this and many of the following stanzas include extensive
   and largely correct explanations of kennings, all of which Percy ignores
   except - in this verse - for *til heimsala Óðins*, 'to Óðinn's home-halls',
   that is, to Valhalla. This is a good example of his policy, enunciated in the
   Preface, 'to substitute a more simple expression instead of the complex
   and enigmatic phrase of the original', except where he could tap into
   concepts that contributed to the general picture of ancient Scandinavia
   that he sought to build up for the reader. Clearly, the cluster of concepts
   that included Óðinn as god of war and slain warriors, Valhalla and the
   valkyries were important to this enterprise, though the last two were not
   yet styled by their Norse names. Percy uses 'Valhall', for the first time
   in English according to the *OED*, both on p. 60 of *Five Pieces* in his
   Introduction to 'The Funeral Song of Hacon' and in *Northern Antiquities*
   I, 87.

[30]

We fought with fwords: the army
caft away their fhields. Then flew the
fpear to the breafts of the warriors.
The fword in the fight cut the very
rocks: the fhield was all befmeared
with blood, before king Rafno fell, our
foe. The warm fweat run down from
the heads on the coats of mail.

1.

We fought with fwords, before the
ifles of Indir. We gave ample prey
for the ravens to rend in pieces: a banquet for the wild beafts that feed on
flefh. At that time all were valiant:
it were difficult to fingle out any one.
At the rifing of the fun, I faw the lances
pierce: the bows darted the arrows from
them.

We fought with fwords: loud was
the

1. Percy's translation here reveals another of his common practices, to substitute a general for a particular reference, partly perhaps to avoid too many notes, partly because he himself is likely to have found the references obscure. His 'The sword in the fight cut the very rocks' is less specific than the Latin gloss *Momordit Scarforum cautes/ Gladius in pugna* and ignores the note, which suggests that the first element of this still unidentified place-name derives from the Icelandic word for a cormorant, *skarfr*. The second element, *sker*, is the source of English *skerry*, but this word seems to have been restricted to Orkney usage or descriptions of the Orkney Islands until the mid-nineteenth century (*OED*, *skerry*, sb., senses 1 a and b), so presumably was inaccessible to Percy. 'the shield was all besmeared with blood' resolutely follows the Latin gloss *Sangvineus erat clypeus* and ignores the shield-kenning *randar máni*, 'moon of the rim', even though it is explained in the notes (with *rǫnd* glossed *umbo*, 'boss'). There are numerous examples throughout his translation where he could have used the notes in Worm to produce a more exact rendering of the Icelandic text, but failed to do so.

[31]

the din * of arms; before king Eiftin
fell in the field. Thence, enriched with
golden fpoils, we marched to fight in
the land of Vals. There the fword cut
the painted fhields †. In the meeting
of helmets, the blood ran from the
wounds: it ran down from the cloven
fculls of men.

We fought with fwords, before Bo-
ring-holmi. We held bloody fhields:
we ftained our fpears. Showers of arrows brake the fhield in pieces. The
bow fent forth the glittering fteel. Volnir fell in the conflict, than whom there
was not a greater king. Wide on the

---

* DIN is the word in the Iflandic original.
    Dinn greniudu brottam.

† Literally, " the paintings of the fhields."

fhores

z

1. I can find no explanation for Percy's reading of *dinn* in this note. In his 'Islandic original' text on p. 89 he gives the reading 'Hett greniudu hrottar', which is also in Worm's version, with the gloss *Altum mugierunt enses*, 'the swords roared loudly'. Modern editors read *hátt* (or *hótt*), 'loudly'. The word must be an adverb, whatever its meaning. Percy's Bodleian notebook has a text of this verse in his hand on f. 12v, and he has glossed some of the words in English, including this one, for which he gives 'height', showing his recognition of its lexical but not its grammatical sense.

2. This note, and that in Worm which Percy follows, is based on the reading of Uppsala University Library R 702, which has *rekyndil sneid randa ritur*. Worm's notes gloss *ritur* as 'pictura, *eg Rita* pingo, scribo; alias *Rit* totam armaturam auro pictam denotat', imagining it to have something to do with writing and painting, hence Percy's note to a reading which is literally 'the corpse-candle [SWORD] cut the pictures of shields' Other manuscripts read *rækyndill smó rauðar/ rítr*, 'the corpse-candle [SWORD] pierced the red shields', *rít* being a poetic word for a shield.

[32]

ſhores lay the ſcattered dead : the wolves rejoiced over their prey.

We fought with ſwords, in the Fle-mings land : the battle widely raged before king Freyr fell therein. The blue ſteel all reeking with blood fell at length upon the golden mail. Many a virgin bewailed the ſlaughter of that morning. The beaſts of prey had ample ſpoil.

We fought with ſwords, before Ain-glanes. There ſaw I thouſands lie dead in the ſhips : we ſailed to the battle for ſix days before the army fell. There we celebrated a *maſs* of weapons *. At

the

___

* This is intended for a ſneer on the Chriſtian religion, which tho' it had not gained any footing in the northern nations, when this Ode was writ-ten, was not wholly unknown to them. Their piratical

1.

1. Percy, like most writers on ancient poetry of his day, considered that such poetry had to be non-Christian in order to be judged authentic. This note indicates that he saw 'savage manners' as incompatible with Christianity. He therefore needed to find an appropriate explanation to account for the existence of the word *messa*, 'mass', 'song', obviously derived from the vocabulary of Christianity, in a supposedly pagan poem, albeit in a battle-kenning *odda messa*, 'the mass of [spear]-points [BATTLE]'. He follows Worm's note in his suggestion that 'this is intended for a sneer on the Christian religion'. A similar note occurs in *Northern Antiquities* II, 145. In fact *messa* appears in some of the earliest skaldic poetry composed by Christian skalds (cf. LP, *messa*).

   Percy has misconstrued the syntax of the latter part of this verse, which should read 'we celebrated a mass of weapons [BATTLE] at the rising of the sun.'

[33]

rifing of the fun Valdiofur fell before our fwords.

We fought with fwords, at Barda-fyrda. A fhower of blood rained from our weapons. Headlong fell the palid corpfe a prey for the hawks. The bow gave a twanging found. The blade fharply bit the coats of mail: it bit the helmet in the fight. The arrow fharp with poifon and all befprinkled with blood fweat ran to the wound.

1.

We fought with fwords, before the bay of Hiadding. We held aloft magic fhields in the play of battle. Then

2.

piratical expeditions into the fouthern countries had given them fome notion of it, but by no means a favourable one: they confidered it as the religion of cowards, becaufe it would have corrected their favage manners.

D   might

1. The rather awkward sense of the last part of this stanza is the product of the ms reading of Uppsala University Library R 702, which has *almur*, 'bow', instead of other mss' *ormr*, 'snake' (metaphorical for sword) in the penultimate line. This makes the rest of the clause, *rendi til unda*, 'ran to the wounds', sound rather odd. Worm's note suggests '*Almur* arcus ponitur pro sagitta'.

2. Percy follows Worm's interlinear translation for 'magic shields' (*magica scuta*), for which there is no authority in the Icelandic text. The idea that the shields were magical comes from the notes to this stanza in Worm, where the valkyrie name *Hlǫkk* in the shield-kenning *Lakkar tjǫld*, 'the tents of Hlǫkk [SHIELDS]' is glossed '*Hlok* in genitivo *Hlokar* magam aut dæmonem notat'.

[34]

might you fee men, who rent fhields
with their fwords. The helmets were
fhattered in the murmur of the warriors. The pleafure of that day was
like having a fair virgin placed befide
one in the bed.

We fought with fwords, in the Nor-
thumbrian land. A furious ftorm de-
fcended on the fhields : many a lifelefs
body fell to the earth. It was about
the time of the morning, when the
foe was compelled to fly in the battle.
There the fword fharply bit the polifh-
ed helmet. The pleafure of that day
was like kiffing a young widow at the
higheft feat of the table.

We fought with fwords, in the ifles
of the fouth. There Herthiofe proved

1.

3   victo-

1. This stanza and the one preceding it were among the most famous in Ragnarr's ode in the eighteenth century, principally on account of the last two lines of each, which seemed to draw a comparison between the activity of fighting battles and the pleasures of sexual adventure. As has been mentioned in the introductory commentary to this poem, the apparent similarity of fighting to wooing was based on a grammatical misunderstanding. In each stanza the Icelandic text has the verbal form *vasat*, 'it was not', with a suffixed negative particle *-at*. This was not understood by early translators, including Worm, who thought the text meant that the pleasures of fighting were like those of wooing. However, Bartholin had the correct meaning (1689, 531), '*Hoc non erat tanquam juvenem viduam/ In primaria sede osculari*'. Interestingly, Percy had copied this correct translation into his notebook (Percy c. 7, f.15r) but written a note to the word *non*, '* NB. *Non* est erratum'! Thus the notion of the Viking warrior approaching battle as if it were a sexual encounter was given renewed life. For a more detailed analysis of these stanzas, see Clunies Ross 1998, 232-236.

116

[35]

victorious: there died many of our valiant warriors.   In the fhower of arms
Rogvaldur fell: I loft my fon.   In the
play of arms came the deadly fpear:
his lofty creft was dyed with gore.
The birds of prey bewailed his fall:
they loft him that prepared them ban-
quets.

We fought with fwords, in the Irifh
plains.   The bodies of the warriors lay
intermingled.   The hawk rejoiced at
the play of fwords.   The Irifh king did
1.   not act the part of the eagle * * *.
Great was the conflict of fword and
fhield.   King Marftan was killed in
the bay: he was given a prey to the
hungry ravens.

We fought with fwords: the fpear
D 2   re-

1. Percy failed to understand this part of the stanza, probably because of its fractured syntax; it should read, 'King Marstan, who governed Ireland, did not allow either eagle or wolf to fast'.

[36]

refounded: the banners fhone * upon
the coats of mail. I faw many a warrior fall in the morning: many a hero
in the contention of arms. Here the
fword reached betimes the heart of my
fon: it was Egill deprived Agnar of
life. He was a youth, who never knew
what it was to fear.

We fought with fwords, at Skioldunga. We kept our words: we carved
out with our weapons a plenteous banquet for the wolves of the fea †. The
fhips were all befmeared with crimfon,
as if for many days the maidens had
brought and poured forth wine. All
rent was the mail in the clath of arms.

* Or more properly " reflected the funfhine up-
" on the coat of mail."

† A poetical name for the fifhes of prey.

We

1. Percy's 'He was a youth, who never knew what it was to fear' is a rather free rendition of the Icelandic *óblauðan hal*, 'the uncowardly man'. Percy does not attempt the last two lines of this stanza, though they appear in Worm, probably because they contain a kenning for a mail-coat, *Hamðis gránserkr*, 'Hamðir's [name of a legendary hero] grey shirt [MAIL-COAT]'. This kenning contains a reference to an heroic legend which Percy either did not understand or did not want to annotate.

2. Percy's note explaining a supposed kenning 'wolves of the sea' [FISHES OF PREY] is based upon a note in Worm's edition, which is ingenious but unlikely to be correct. This part of the stanza reads *Haldorða sák brytja/ ekki smátt fyr ulfa/ Endils niðja brondum*, 'I saw men true to their word carve Endill's [sea-king] kinsmen [SEA-WARRIORS] into large pieces with swords for the wolves' (or possibly, as Finnur Jónsson has it (*Skjald* B I, 653), 'I saw Endill's resolute kinsmen carve [men] into large pieces with swords for the wolves'.

   The mistranslation 'The ships were all besmeared with crimson, as if for many days the maidens had brought and poured forth wine', is based upon a similar misunderstanding in Worm and is yet another instance where a negated verb *vasat* has been understood to introduce a positive comparison between domestic comfort and the tough life of a Viking. The poet of *Krákumál* makes considerable use of this kind of contrast, its purpose being to stress the absence of soft domestic comforts in the lives of warriors on the Viking path.

[37]

1.

We fought with fwords; when Harold fell. I faw him ftrugling in the
twilight of death; that young chief fo
proud of his flowing locks *: he who
fpent his mornings among the young
maidens: he who loved to converfe
with the handfome widows. * * * *

We fought with fwords: we fought
three kings in the ifle of Lindis. Few
had reafon to rejoice that day. Many
fell into the jaws of the wild-beafts.
The hawk and the wolf tore the flefh
of the dead: they departed glutted with
their prey. The blood of the Irifh fell
plentifully into the ocean, during the
time of that flaughter.

* He means Harold Harfax king of Norway.—
Harfax (fynonymous to our Englifh *Fairfax*) fignifies *Fair-locks*.

1. Percy found the suggestion that this stanza referred to the death of the Norwegian king Haraldr hárfagri in Worm's notes. Although the adjective *hárfagr*, 'with fine, beautiful hair' appears in line 2 of the Icelandic text, the reference is quite general and is unlikely to refer to King Haraldr, *Hárfagran sák røkkva/ meyjar dreng of morgin/ ok málvini ekkju*, 'I saw the maiden's beautiful-haired young man and the widow's confidant grow dark in the morning'. The rest of Percy's stanza is sublime and romantic, again supported (but only in part) by Worm's gloss, which yet again fails to understand the suffixed negative -*at* in *vasat*. The trope here is similar to the one in the verse above, *vasat sem varmar laugar/ ví nkers Njǫrun bæri/ oss í Álasundi*, 'it was not in Álasund as if the Njǫrun [goddess] of the wine-cask [WOMAN] were to bring us warm baths'. Percy's note on Harold 'Harfax' seems to represent a confusion of some information that Edward Lye had given him. A note in Lye's hand is inserted on a slip of paper between pages 50 and 51 of Volume 2 of Percy's copy of the first edition of Mallet, now in the Rare Book Library of The Queen's University, Belfast (No. 288). It reads 'p. 50: Harold Harfagre/ see Hair in Jun./ Har and fax are/ synonimous.' In his own copy of *Five Pieces*, also in The Queen's University Library Belfast, Percy has noted 'sed vide finem' beside his footnote to p. 37 and added an Erratum on the blank leaf that follows the last page of printed text, 'In Page 37. Note and/ in Pag. 59 &c./ For *Harold Harfax*, read *Harold Harfagre*. *Harfagre*, is compounded of the Icelandic Words *Har*, Hair,/ and *fagre* fair. – *Har*, and/ *Fax* are synonymous: both of them signify Hair, or/ Locks.'

[38]

We fought with fwords, at the ifle
of Onlug.   The uplifted weapon bit the
fhields.   The gilded lance grated on the
mail.   The traces of that fight will be
feen for ages.   There kings marched
up to the play of arms.   The fhores of
the· fea were ftained with blood.   The
lances appeared like flying dragons.

We fought with fwords.   Death is
the happy portion of the brave * ; for
he ftands the foremoft againft the ftorm
of weapons.   He, who flies from danger,
often bewails his miferable life.   Yet
how difficult is it to rouze up a coward
to the play of arms ?   The daftard feels
no heart in his bofom.

---

* The northern warriors thought none were
intitled to Elizium, but fuch as died in battle, or
underwent a violent death.

We

1. 'at the isle of Onlug': Percy's name for the Icelandic *Ǫngulsey*, probably Anglesey, derives from Worm's Latin gloss, *in Onlugs insula*. The Latin notes give the correct form, and suggest the name is that of an island in the Orkneys. The last sentence, 'The lances appeared like flying dragons' is based upon the note to the spear-kenning *flugdreki sára*, 'flying dragon of wounds', 'hasta, quæ est quasi vulnerum volans draco'.

[39]

We fought with fwords. Young men
fhould march up to the conflict of
arms: man fhould meet man and never
give way. In this hath always con-
fifted the nobility of the warrior. He,
who afpires to the love of his miftrefs,
ought to be dauntlefs in the clafh of
arms.

We fought with fwords. Now I
find for certain that we are drawn
along by fate. Who can evade the de-
1.   crees of deftiny? Could I have thought
the conclufion of my life referved for
Ella; when almoft expiring I fhed tor-
2.   rents of blood? When I launched forth
my fhips into the deep? When in the
Scotifh gulphs I gained large fpoils for
the wolves?

D 4   We

1. The reference in the Icelandic text is to the decrees of the Norns (*skǫp Norna*), three female figures who decide men's fates in Norse mythology. Worm's gloss and notes do not illuminate the text here, beyond the gloss *fata Parcarum* and the explanation '*Skop* dicuntur a *Scopur* creatio, quasi Parcæ prospera & adversa homini concreent.' According to the *OED*, *norn* sb. [1], Percy was the first to use the word 'norn' in English in the form 'nornies', but not until *Northern Antiquities* (1770 II, 51): 'These [virgins] are they who dispense the ages of men; they are called Nornies, that is, Fairies or Destinies'.
2. Percy follows a misunderstanding in the Worm gloss here. The Icelandic reads *þás blóðvali bræddak*, 'when I gave food to the blood-falcon [RAVEN]', which the Latin glosses as 'cum ego sangvinem semimortuus tegerem'.

[40]

1.

2.

We fought with fwords : this fills
me ftill with joy, becaufe I know a
banquet is preparing by the father of
the gods. Soon, in the fplendid hall
of Odin, we fhall drink Beer * out of
the fculls of our enemies. A brave
man fhrinks not at death. I fhall utter
no repining words as I approach the
palace of the gods.

We fought with fwords. O that the
fons of Aflauga † knew; O that my
children knew the fufferings of their father! that numerous ferpents filled with
poifon tear me to pieces! Soon would

* Beer and Mead were the only nectar of the
northern nations. Odin alone of all the gods was
fuppofed to drink Wine. *Vid. Bartholin.*

† Aflauga was his fecond wife, whom he married after the death of Thora.

they

1. In spite of the fact that both Latin gloss and notes in Worm, not to speak of the Icelandic text, have the Óðinn-kenning *Baldrs faðir*, 'Baldr's father', here, Percy does not include the precise mythological reference. For him, evidently, Baldr had not become an object of romantic fascination, as he was for Victorian readers.

2. It has already been noted that this famous sublime image is based on a misunderstanding of the Icelandic text, which reads *drekkum bjór af bragði/ ór bjúgviðum hausa*, 'we shall soon drink beer from the curved trees of skulls [DRINKING HORNS]'. Worm's notes are the basis for the erroneous interpretation we find in Percy and many other eighteenth-century translators: *Sperabant Heroes se in aula Othini bibituros ex craniis eorum quos occiderant.*

[41]

they be here : foon would they wage
bitter war with their fwords. I gave
a mother to my children from whom
they inherit a valiant heart.

We fought with fwords. Now I touch
on my laft moments. I receive a deadly hurt from the viper. A ferpent in-
habits the hall of my heart. Soon fhall
my fons black their fwords in the blood
of Ella. They wax red with fury :
they burn with rage. Thofe gallant
youths will not reft till they have a-
venged their father.

We fought with fwords. Battles fifty
and one have been fought under my
banners. From my early youth I learnt
to dye my fword in crimfon : I never
yet could find a king more valiant than
myfelf.

1. The colour word in this dramatic image and the next, representing Ragnarr's sons as 'wax[ing] red with fury', derive from the Latin translation in Worm, and are not in the Icelandic text.

[42]

myfelf. The gods now invite me to
them. Death is not to be lamented.

'Tis with joy I ceafe. The god-
deffes of deftiny are come to fetch me.
Odin hath fent them from the habitation of the gods. I fhall be joyfully
received into the higheft feat; I fhall
quaff full goblets among the gods. The
hours of my life are paft away. I die
1. laughing.

THE

1. This famous final stanza includes several key images of Viking ideology, as eighteenth-century people imagined it. The brave hero, having suffered torment, acknowledges the power of 'the goddesses of destiny' (*dísir*) and looks forward to being transported by them to Óðinn's halls in Valhalla, there to enjoy his ale. Percy knew the term *valkyrie*, which he had written into his notebook when copying out Bartholin's version of this stanza, with the note to *Disæ*, 'Disas pro Valkyriis nuncupat' (Percy c. 7, f. 16r). He was later to use it, and the word Valhall, in *Northern Antiquities* (I, 102).

    There are a few minor embellishments or errors in the final lines of this stanza: *ǫl*, 'ale', becomes 'full goblets', and *lífs eru liðnar vánir*, 'hopes of life have passed away' becomes 'the hours of my life are past away' (which depends on the Latin in Worm's gloss).

(III.)

THE

RANSOME

OF

EGILL the SCALD.

'The Ransome of Egill the Scald', or *Hǫfuðlausn* ('Head-ransom') as it is usually now known, follows *Krákumál* in the Appendix to Ole Worm's *Literatura Runica*, and this was Percy's main source. Here there was a parallel Icelandic and Latin translation, not an interlinear Latin gloss, as was the case with 'The Dying Ode of Regner Lodbrog'. Percy was also familiar with Bartholin's discussion of the poem. His notebook (Bodleian MS Percy c. 7) contains transcripts of stanzas 1-7 in Worm's version (but not in runes) on f. 28r and stanza 5 and lines from stanzas 1 and 2 transcribed from Bartholin on f. 29v. Mallet did not publish a text of the poem, but mentioned it in the section of his *Introduction à l'Histoire de Dannemark* that discusses the role and status of poets, specially skaldic poets, in ancient Scandinavia. Percy notes this reference (to the first edition of Mallet) in his own Introduction to the poem. There are a few notes and glosses to this poem by Edward Lye in Percy c. 7, ff. 36r and 38r. 'The Ransome of Egill the Scald' is Smith 1989, PeT 21 and 92 and Clunies Ross 1998, 87, no. 3.

Hǫfuðlausn is attributed to the celebrated Icelandic Viking Age skald Egill Skallagrímsson and has been preserved in some manuscripts of *Egils saga*. It belongs to a genre of skaldic verse in which a poet redeems himself from punishment or death at the hands of a ruler or patron because of a misdemeanour by composing a flattering praise-poem in the ruler's honour. In Chapter 60 of *Egils saga* the narrative tells how Egill, after a long and bitter conflict with King Eiríkr blóðøx ('blood-axe') of Norway and his Queen Gunnhildr, in the course of which the king was driven out of Norway, is drawn to the king's new seat of power at York by means of the queen's sorcery. He is brought into the king's hall where his life is at risk, as he has been the cause of Eiríkr's banishment and has killed one of his sons. However, his friend Arinbjǫrn intercedes with the king on his behalf, and Egill is given the opportunity to ransom his head by composing a suitably flattering poem about Eiríkr. *Hǫfuðlausn* is the result. The poem was known in the European literary world long before the saga itself, though summary accounts of the supposed circumstances of its production were available in Worm, Bartholin and some other secondary sources. A printed edition of *Egils saga* did not appear until 1809, when an edition and translation, probably by Grímur Jónsson Thorkelín, was published in Copenhagen. The first English translation of the saga seems to have been by W. C. G[reen] in 1893.

There were three reasons why Percy was attracted to this poem, aside from the availability of its text in Worm's Appendix. The first is that the poem, and the story of Egill himself, so far as it was then known, exemplified the high regard in which poetry was held among the ancient Scandinavians and the important role of the court poet or skald, both of which were significant elements in Percy's representation of the nature and high status of poetry and poets in supposedly primitive societies. The second reason is that the poem was said to have been composed and performed in England, while Eiríkr ruled the Viking kingdom of York (he was expelled in 954). This context meant that Percy and his English readers could make special claim to this poem as part of their own cultural history, just as they could with 'The Dying Ode of Regner Lodbrog'. The third reason why Percy valued *Hǫfuðlausn* was because of its verse-form. It was composed in *runhent*, a verse-form that uses end rhyme, unlike most other skaldic measures where internal rhyme and assonance, in addition to alliteration, ornament the verse. We have already seen that Percy mentioned the significance of 'Egils Ode' as proof that rhyme came into European poetry from Scandinavia in his Preface to *Five Pieces*.

Allowing for the fact that Worm (and therefore Percy) made use of a text of *Hǫfuðlausn* that was rather different in many of its manuscript readings and verse sequences from those favoured by modern editors, their versions of this poem are significantly inferior in terms of closeness to the Old Icelandic compared with their renderings of *Krákumál*. The reason for this almost certainly lies in the abundance of kennings in *Hǫfuðlausn* in comparison with *Krákumál*. These kennings are not complex in form, but the special poetic words that they employ are often misinterpreted or the kenning referent is misunderstood in Worm's translation and notes, and this leads Percy astray.

The following page, D6b, is blank.

[45]

INTRODUCTION.

" **T**HE following piece is an il-
" luftrious proof of the high re-
" verence in which poets and their art
" were held among the northern na-
" tions. It was compofed by Egill a
" celebrated *Scald* or poet, who having
" received fome injury from Eric Blo-
" dox king of Norway, had in revenge
" killed his fon and feveral of his friends.
" Being afterwards feized in Iceland by
" Eric's queen, fhe fent him after her
1. " hufband into England; which he
" had juft before invaded, and where
" he then had gained fome footing.
" Though Egill had fo highly exaf-
" perated the king, he purchafed his
" pardon by the poem, here tranflated;

2   " which,

1. According to the saga, Egill was drawn to England by Gunnhildr's powers of sorcery, which prevented him from enjoying peace of mind in Iceland.

[46]

" which, notwithſtanding it is all in
" rhyme, and conſiſts of a great va-
" riety of meaſures; and tho' the ſtyle
" is uncommonly figurative, is ſaid to
" have been pronounced extempore in
" a full aſſembly of Eric and his
" chiefs."

    Mallet Introd. a l'Hiſt. de Dannem. p.
247. *Olaij Worm. Lit. Run. p.* 195.

    " The tranſlation is made from the
" Iſlandic original, publiſhed by Olaus
" Wormius in his *Literatura Runica*,
" 4*to. pag.* 227.

    " N. B. In the following poem Eric
" is called THE ENGLISH CHIEF, in
" compliment to his having gained ſome
" footing in the kingdom of Northum-
                            " berland.

1.

1. Percy's interpretation here is based upon a mistranslation in Worm; see
   note to stanza 2.

[47]

" berland.———He is alſo intitled THE
" COMMANDER OF THE FLEET OF
" SCOTS ; from his having auxiliaries
" of that nation : it was uſual for the
" Scots to join the Danes &c. in their
" irruptions into the ſouthern parts of
" the iſland."

THE

The following page, D8b, is blank.

[49]

THE

R A N S O M E

OF

EGILL the SCALD.

1. I Came by fea from the weft. I bring in my bofom the gift of Odin. Thus was my paffage: I launched into the ocean in fhips of Iceland: my mind is deep laden with the fongs of the gods.

2. I offer my freight unto the king: I owe a poem for my ranfome. I prefent to the Englifh chief the fongs of Odin. Renown is imperfect without fongs. My lays refound his praife; I

E   intreat

1. Percy's translation is tolerably accurate, though 'I launched into the ocean in ships of Iceland' misses part of the meaning of *drók eik á flot/ við ísa brot*, 'I drew the oak afloat at the breaking of the ice, i.e. in spring', translated in Worm as *Deduxi ego quercum in mare/ Apud Islandiam.* Percy changes the first poetry-kenning *Viðris munstrandar mar*, 'Viðir's [=Óðinn's] mind-shore sea' [MOUTH > POETRY] to a more readily comprehensible type, 'the gift of Odin', while the second, which is complicated by a metaphorical analogy with loading cargo aboard a ship, becomes 'my mind is deep laden with the songs of the gods', which stresses poetry's divine connections in line with Percy's views of ancient verse and the suggested paraphrase in Worm's notes, *navis me huc vexit, at ego in pectore veho Poema.* Worm's text read *minnis* not *míns* in the last line of this stanza, as most modern editors prefer: *hlóðk mærðar hlut/ míns knarrar skut*, 'I loaded the stern of my ship with a portion of praise'.

2. Percy follows the incorrect interpretation of *á Engla bjǫð,* 'to the land of the English' as 'to the English chief', which he finds in Worm's translation and notes, *In Anglorum Regem, Biod præcipiens seu Rex a verbo ad bioda imperare, præcipere.* He changes the poetry-kenning *Óðins mjǫð,* 'Óðinn's mead', which Worm translates correctly, to the rather pallid 'the songs of Odin'. 'Renown is imperfect without songs' is just a guess for *lofat vísa vann.*

[50]

intreat his filent attention; while he is
the fubject of my fong.

Liften, O prince, that I may fwell
the ftrain.   If I can obtain but filence,
many men fhall know the atchieve-
1.   ments of the king.   Odin hath feen
where the dead bodies lie.

The clafh of arms increafed about
the edges of the fhield.   The god-
2.   deffes of war had required this of him.
The king was impetuous: he was dif-
tinguifhed in the tumult: a torrent
3.   flowed from his fword: the ftorm of
weapons furioufly raged.

The web of fpears went furioufly
forward; thro' the refounding ranks of
4.   fhields; among the carcaffes deftined to
glad

1. The Icelandic text has *Viðrir*, one of Óðinn's many names. Worm gives *Odinus* here.
2. Percy's rendition here follows Worm's translation and gloss, which is based on a different manuscript reading (*vogs* or *vox* for *óx*) in the line which modern editors read as *guðr óx of gram*, 'battle grew round the prince'. Worm's translation is *Deæ militiæ requisiverant de rege*, and the note, '*Gudor vox* Dea quædam Asiatica, quæ multiscia fingitur, adeo ut nemini integrum sit quid quam aggredi quod eam latere possit, vide Eddam'.
3. Percy has attempted to convey the sense of the kenning in *þaut mækis ó*, 'the river of the sword resounded', without actually translating it. Normally this would be a blood-kenning, as Worm's note points out, but in this context seems more likely to allude to the noise of battle.
4. It is interesting that Percy gives the correct lexical sense of line 2 of the Icelandic, *vefr darraðar*, 'web of spears' here, even though Worm's translation interprets Darraðr as a proper name, referring to the episode in Ch. 157 of *Njáls saga* (but not identifying it precisely) in which a man by that name is said to have observed a group of valkyries weaving a magic web presaging the deaths of warriors while chanting the poem *Darraðarljóð*, which Percy also translated (see below, *Two translations of Darraðarljóð*). Worm's note suggests '*Vefur Darader* id est mors'. F. 29v of Percy's Bodleian notebook indicates that he knew and had copied out the reference in Bartholin (1689, 624), which makes the connection between the use of *vefr darraðar* in both Egill's *Hǫfuðlausn* and *Darraðarljóð* and gives its correct meaning, pointing out that the author of *Njáls saga* misinterpreted the word *darraðr* as a proper name. Percy seems to have forgotten this last observation (and in fact did not copy it into his notebook) when he translated *Darraðarljóð* (see below, pp. 251 and 264). Edward Lye seems to have been consulted on the subject. He explains in a note 'darraþur exponitur Gladius' (Percy c. 7, f. 36r), though this could be a reference to the occurrence of *darraðr* in *Hákonarmál* 2, where both Peringskiöld and Percy translate the word as 'sword' (see 'The Funeral Song of Hacon', verse 2).

   'went furiously forward', based loosely on Worm's *pergebat avij loci*, is a misunderstanding of *Varat villr* (Worm, *villu*) *staðar*, '[the web of spears, BATTLE] was not out of place'.

   In the following line, the adjective 'resounding' mistranslates the Icelandic *glaðr*, though Worm gives its sense correctly, but misunderstands the kenning in the following line, so making Percy's translation difficult.

[51]

1.   glad the eagles. The ſhip ſailed in a ſea of blood. Wounds reſounded on all ſides.

2.   The feet of the warriors failed at the diſcharge of arrows. There Eric acquired deathleſs renown.

3.
4.   I ſhall proceed if the warriors will liſten: I have heard of all their glorious renown. The wounds boiled at the king's attack. The ſwords were broken againſt the azure ſhields.

The broken harneſs gave a craſh: the helmets flaſhed out fire. Sharp was the ſword: it was a bloody deſtroyer. I know that many warriors

1. There are several difficulties in the second half of this stanza, and some major differences between manuscripts. Worm's translation and notes would not have helped Percy much, though he tries to follow them. For a discussion of some of the problems associated with this half-stanza, see Nordal 1933, 187.

2. In his 'Islandic original' (pp. 92-5), Percy has followed Worm's text in marking the various sections of the poem, which, by virtue of having a refrain or *stef*, is classified as a *drápa*. This is the first of four refrain verses, a larger than usual space between stanzas marking the different sections in this translation. Percy's 'deathless renown' for *orðstírr*, 'word-glory' [RENOWN], is an attempt to make sense of Worm's gloss to the word, whose second element he attempts to relate to the name of the Norse god Týr.

3. Percy's translation embroiders the Icelandic *frǫgum fleira/ til frama þeira*, 'we have heard more about their courage'.

4. Percy, following Worm, was translating *ǫstusk undir*, 'wounds were stirred up, made violent'. Other manuscripts read *óxu undir*, 'wounds increased'. There seems to be some uncertainty about the manuscript readings of this and the following line, as, without emendation, they do not rhyme (see Nordal 1933, 187-8). Worm's text actually emends the second line of the couplet to *fundir*, plural of *fundr*, 'meeting, battle' from mss *fundi* and indicates this in the notes, though Percy does not seem to recognise the sense of the emendation in his translation.

[52]

fell before the fpringing bow, in the play of weapons.

Then was there a devouring of fpears, in the clafh of arms. There Eric acquired deathlefs renown.

The king dyed his fword in crimfon; his fword that glutted the hungry ravens. The weapon aimed at human life. The bloody lances flew. The commander of the Scotifh fleet fed fat the birds of prey. The fifter of Nara* trampled on the foe: fhe trampled on the evening food of the eagle.

* An Iflandic phrafe for death, it alludes to the ancient northern mythology. See the EDDA, &c.

The

1. Although its syntax is simple, this stanza contains a number of kennings, most of them for the sword. Of the seven kennings here, in only one, the last and least unusual, does Percy attempt to give the reader an idea of the original and even here he substitutes a general 'play of weapons' for the *járnleikr*, 'iron play' [BATTLE] of the Icelandic. In some cases he, following Worm, misunderstands the kennings, in others turns them into general statements. Thus, in the order in which they occur in the verse, *heinsǫðull*, 'hone-saddle' [SWORD] becomes 'the broken harness' (this kenning was misunderstood in Worm); *hjálmrǫðull* (reading of Worm), 'helmet-sun' [?SWORD] becomes 'the helmets flashed out fire'; *beit bengrefill*, 'the wound engraver [SWORD] bit' becomes 'sharp was the sword'; *þat var blóðrefill*, 'that was a blood-point' [SWORD POINT, barely a kenning], is 'it was a bloody destroyer'. *Fetilsvell*, 'belt-icesheet' [SWORD] is mistranslated (as it is in Worm) as 'the springing bow', while *Óðins eiki*, 'Óðinn's oak-wood' [WARRIORS] becomes 'many warriors'.

2. This curious expression is based on the interpretative note in Worm to *Þar var odda at*, 'There was a clash of spear points', in which the noun *at* is glossed '*at proprie concitatio est*'.

3. Worm's *præcipiens classis Scotorum* is an effort to understand a kenning for King Eiríkr, in which the first element was given as *Tharbiodur skota*, and glossed as '*Thar* navis'. Modern editors choose the reading *fárbjóðr*, 'danger-offerer, i.e. opponent [of the Scots]'. Worm's notes misunderstand the referent of the wolf-kenning *flagðs goti*, 'giantess's horse' [WOLF], which he interprets as a kenning for birds of prey, hence Percy's translation.

4. *Nipt Nara*, 'sister of Nari' is a kenning for Hel, custodian of the underworld, to which place the dead who do not die in battle travel after death. Hel is the daughter of the god Loki by a giantess, Angrboða. Nari is the name of one of Loki's sons by his goddess wife Sigyn, and thus the half-brother of Hel.

[53]

1. The beaked lances flew amidſt the edges of the ſword. The weapons accuſtomed to meaſure wounds were imbrued in blood. The wolf mangled the feſtering wounds. Over their prey
2. the ravens tumultuouſly aſſembled.

3. The dreadful inundation overwhelmed the ſecure. Eric gave the dead bodies to the wolves in the ſea *.

Sharp was the flying dart : then peace was loſt. Bent was the bow; at which the wolf rejoiced. Broken were the lances. Sharp were the ſwords. The
4. bow-ſtrings bare away the arrows.

5. * An Islandic phraſe for fiſhes of prey.

E 3   The

1. Percy follows Worm's misunderstanding of the kenning *hjaldrs tranar*, 'cranes of battle' as a weapon-kenning (though Worm in fact offers a correct reading of each of the kenning elements). It is more likely that it refers to eagles or other birds of prey than to weapons.

2. There are several difficulties in Percy's translation of the remainder of this stanza, which follows Worm for the most part. These difficulties are partly attributable to different manuscript readings. Worm's text in line 4 has *ben-mal-granar*, for *ben mós granar*, 'wound-gulls' [RAVENS'] beaks'; this produces Percy's unfortunate 'the weapons accustomed to measure wounds'. Of Percy's last two sentences, the first is made more grisly by the addition of the adjective 'festering', not in the Icelandic, while the second is again dependent on a Worm translation and variant manuscript reading (*hǫfuðtafn*, 'head-prey/sacrifice', 'primariam & magnam prædam cadaverum') not *hǫfuðstafn*, 'head-prow' [BEAK], as most modern editors construe the kenning, giving a general sense to the last three lines of 'and the spearpoint-wave [BLOOD] splashed onto the raven's head-prow [BEAK]'.

3. Percy again strives to make sense of Worm's readings here, which give a rather different sense from the text preferred by most modern editors, *kom gríðar læl at Gjalpar skæ*, 'the destruction of hunger [SATIETY] came for Gjalp's [giantess] steed [WOLF].' Worm reads *grydar skiae*, 'securis nocumentum' and *galfrar lae*, 'mare', respectively for these two kennings.

4. In Worm's text this verse was a combination of lines from what modern editors number as stanzas 14 (1-4) and 13 (5-8).

5. The couplet means rather 'Eiríkr offered corpses to wolves by the sea', and there is no kenning here. Percy has mistranscribed Worm's runic *ulfum* here as *ulfur* (p. 94), which is impossible grammatically.

[54]

The valiant provoker of warlike play
fends the lances from his hand : he is
prodigal of blood. It is poured forth
on all fides. The fong flows from my
heart. The expedition of Eric is celebrated thro' the eaftern ocean.

1.

2.

The king bent his bow : the ftinging
arrows fly. Eric gave the dead bodies
to the wolves in the fea.

3.

It remains that I diftinguifh among
the warriors the fuperior excellence of
the king. My fong will flow more rapid. He caufes the goddefs of war to
watch upon his prow. He makes his
fhip to fcate along the rough billows.

The

1. In modern editions, this stanza is number 18. We find here the usual
    obliteration of kennings, some by Worm, others by Percy alone. Thus the
    first clause is based on the Icelandic *Verpr broddfleti/ Með baugseti*, 'he
    moves the spearpoint-surface [SHIELD] with the ring-seat [ARM]. 'he is
    prodigal of blood' is based on Worm's reading *blodskate* instead of
    baugskati, 'ring-generous'. This leads to the improbable 'It is poured forth
    on all sides' (which Worm also has) instead of '[his reputation] increases
    here as everywhere else' for *þróask hér sem hvar*.
2. This refrain stanza is number 15 in modern editors' texts of *Hǫfuðlausn*.
    Whereas Percy would not have known from Worm that *ýr* means a bow
    made of yew wood, Worm's translation and notes alerted him to the
    delightful arrow-kenning *unda bý*, 'wound-bees' (*vulnerum apes*), which,
    however, he turns into a standard English epithet plus noun construction,
    'stinging arrows'. In his 'Icelandic original' on p. 94, Percy has omitted
    the word *ý* ('yew-bow') altogether at the end of the first line of this stanza,
    though it is there in Worm's runic text.
3. Worm's text here comprises lines 1-4 of stanza 16 followed by lines 1-4
    of stanza 13, according to modern editions. There are substantial variations
    in the text of Worm's version, particularly in the second half-stanza. 'He
    causes the goddess of war to watch upon his prow' is based upon a reading
    in Worm *Laetur snot-saka/ Um sud fri vaka*, in which the meaning 'ship'
    is proposed for *súð*. The majority manuscript reading here is *Lætr snót
    saka/ sverð-Frey vaka*, 'the sword-Freyr [god] [WARRIOR] causes the
    woman of contests [VALKYRIE] to wake' (or, less probably, 'the valkyrie
    causes the warrior to wake'). The last sentence is also based upon a set of
    substantially different readings in Worm, translated as *Sed per scopuli
    aratrum/ Navim strepere*. Modern editors see a complex kenning in these
    two lines, *en skers Haka/ skíðgarð braka*, '[the warrior, viz. Eiríkr, caused]
    the ski-fence of Haki's [sea-king] skerry [SEA>SHIP>ROW OF SHIELDS] to
    crack'.

[55]

The king, who breaks the fhower
of arrows, abounds in wealth. The
fhield-rending warriors refound his
praife: the jocund mariners are glad-
dened with his gold: precious ftones
1.   court the hand of the king.

There was no ftanding for the deluge of blood. The drawn bow twangs:
it fends forth the arrow to meet the
fword. The king hath gained a firm
poffeffion in his enemies land. Praife
2.   dwells befide him.

The king hath been attentive to my
lays fuch as I could produce. I am
happy that I could obtain a filent hear-
ing. I have employed my tongue. I

1. Worm's version of this stanza again contains significant variations from other texts, and he reverses the order of lines 5-8 so that, in comparison with modern editions, lines 7-8 become 5-6, and 5-6 become 7-8. Percy's 'shower of arrows' derives from Worm's *bog huita*, glossed as 'arcus pluvia', rather than the *uita* > *bógvita*, 'arm-beacon' [GOLD] favoured by modern editors, though it is a minority manuscript reading. The remainder of Percy's translation of this stanza follows Worm's text, though as usual he replaces the kennings (most of which are gold-kennings and are explained in the notes) with nouns or adjective-plus-noun combinations. Most modern editors select manuscript readings for this stanza that give a series of conventional variations upon the idea that Eiríkr is a generous ruler who distributes gold freely to his men.

2. This stanza in Worm's text represents a sequence of stanza 14, lines 5-8, and stanza 16, 5-8, as they are set out in most modern editions. However, it should be noted that most manuscripts show considerable variability both in wording and sequencing of lines here and it is difficult to establish a preferred sequence and text. There are many variant readings in Worm from those accepted by modern editors. Percy's 'The king hath gained a firm possession in his enemies land' is based rather tenuously on Worm's long note on the text's *enn jǫfurr lǫndum* [Worm *lodum*]/ *heldr hornklofi*, the last word of which is interpreted as a proper name, '*Hornklofe* horn est angulus *klof* incisura, Hornklof dicta videtur regio ubi aulam habuit Rex, quia in sinu quodam & angulo maris sita erat.' On possible meanings of the word *hornklofi*, see Nordal 1933, 190-1.

[56]

have poured forth from my foul the fongs of Odin in this fplendid city.

I have publifhed the praifes of the king: I have broke through the fetters of filence: I have not feared to fpeak in the affembly of warriors. I have poured forth from my breaft the praifes of Eric. They flowed forth that many might hear them.

May he abound in gold. May he enrich his fubjects. May his fame be fpread abroad. May all things fucceed to the king's defires *.

* The laft ftanza is in the orginal fo highly figurative, and contains fuch obfcure allufions to the northern mythology, that it would only admit of a very loofe paraphrafe. That here given, is founded on the notes of Olaus Wormius. pag. 140.

THE

1. This verse is numbered 19 by modern editors. Percy's 'The king hath been
    attentive' departs from the imperative mood indicated by both the Icelandic
    text and Worm's translation. The last part of Percy's version is based on
    Worm's translation and notes. The latter detects a reference to York, in its
    Old Norse form Jórvík, in the last line of the stanza, hence Percy's reference
    to 'this splendid city'. Modern editors prefer to find a kenning for Eiríkr
    here, *jǫru fægir*, 'practitioner of battle'. As usual, Percy avoids translating
    the kennings. Worm's note gives a good explanation for the poetry-kenning
    Óðins ægi, 'Óðinn's sea', in line 7 in the context of a short discussion of
    the underpinning myth of the mead of poetry, but even this does not tempt
    Percy.
2. This stanza, usually numbered 20, is considered by most modern editors
    to be the final stanza of *Hǫfuðlausn*, even though an additional half-stanza
    is found in several manuscripts, and is printed by Worm. Percy's kenning-
    like 'the fetters of silence' has no exact parallel in the Icelandic text, which
    has 'the breaking of silence', *þagnar rof*. The interpretation of this phrase,
    which, if it is a kenning, is an unusual one, is uncertain; it may mean 'that
    which breaks silence', i.e. speech, or the quiet needed for Egill to gain the
    king's attention with his poem. The mind- or breast-kenning *hlátra hamr*,
    'covering of laughter', in line 5 becomes the simple 'my breast' in Percy's
    translation, following the note in Worm.
3. Finnur Jónsson B I, 33 writes that this last half-stanza is incomprehensible
    and without doubt a younger addition to the text. Percy's note seems to
    agree with him. See further Nordal 1933, 192-3 and references cited there.
    The lines contain allusions to the mythological figures Bragi, Vili and
    either Freyja or Óðinn, and seem to advert to myths about gold.

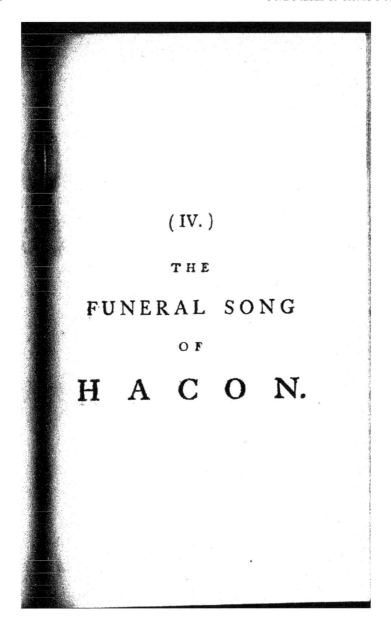

(IV.)

THE

FUNERAL SONG

OF

H A C O N.

'The Funeral Song of Hacon' or, as Percy first referred to it in correspondence with William Shenstone, 'The Epicedium of Haco', was probably one of the first Old Norse poems, if not the first, that he attempted to translate. Full details are presented in the *Introduction* and in *Translations from the works of Viking Age skalds* to show that Percy started to work on his translation of this poem in late 1760, and about the same time translated several skaldic fragments that he found, together with 'The Funeral Song of Hacon', in Johan Peringskiöld's edition (1697, 162-7) of Snorri Sturluson's *Heimskringla* (c.1230), which Percy had probably borrowed from Edward Lye. The verses are cited in manuscripts of Snorri's *Hákonar saga góða* and some are also found in the compilation *Fagrskinna* and in Snorri's *Edda*. Some time later, Percy collated the text in Peringskiöld with that which he found in Bartholin 1689, 520-8 and also consulted Mallet's translation and notes (1756, 159-61). His translation, the first of this poem into English, remains largely indebted to Peringskiöld however, except in a very small number of instances. There are notes and draft translations of the poem from Peringskiöld's edition on ff. 26r-27v and on 30r-31v (Bartholin's version) of Bodleian MS Percy c. 7. Peringskiöld's edition had an Icelandic text and parallel Swedish translation, with a Latin version at the bottom of the page, while Bartholin embeds his Icelandic text with subjoined Latin translation in the general Latin text of his treatise. 'The Funeral Song of Hacon' is Smith 1989 PeT 21 and 27 and Clunies Ross 1998, 87, no. 4.

The poem is known to modern scholars as *Hákonarmál*, 'Talk about Hákon', and is attributed to the tenth-century Norwegian skald Eyvindr Finnsson skáldaspillir (lit. 'the poet destroyer'), who was a court poet of the Norwegian king Hákon góði ('the good') Haraldsson, younger son of Haraldr hárfagri ('fine hair') and half-brother of Eiríkr blóðøx ('blood axe'), for whom Egill Skallagrímsson is said to have composed his *Hǫfuðlausn*. Hákon was fostered at the court of King Æthelstan of England - another English connection for Percy - and was brought up a Christian, but his attempts to introduce the new religion in Norway were unsuccessful and it appears that he left the Christian faith, at least for reasons of political expediency. *Hákonarmál* is a panegyric for Hákon, composed presumably after the king's death at the hands of the sons of Eiríkr in 961. The poem invokes many of the trappings of Norse mythology, first representing the dead king's death in battle, then his dialogue with valkyries who have come to deliver him into Óðinn's hands in Valhalla, and finally Hákon's welcome in Valhalla among the gods. It concludes on a sombre note, however, looking ahead to the destruction of the world at Ragnarǫk and referring to the desperate plight of the people of Norway under the rule of the good king Hákon's successor.

For Percy, and indeed for Mallet and others who presented versions of this poem, it seemed to exemplify many of the core ideas and striking mythological images of ancient Scandinavia, brave warriors fighting, their fates decided by valkyries, and the furniture and actors of the warriors' paradise, Valhalla. Modern scholars have, however, detected a nuanced attitude to these things in the poem, perhaps prompted by its composition in memory of a king brought up a Christian, and known for his fair government, but having to ally himself with one of the most assertively pagan groups in Norway, the Jarls of Hlaðir, in order to survive against his political opponents, the sons of Eiríkr, who were supported by the Danish king (see further Marold 1993a and references cited there).

Hákonarmál is in two poetic verse-forms usually classified as eddic, though eddic measures are also used in skaldic poetry, particularly panegyric and genealogical verse. The first part, describing the battle in which Hákon lost his life, is in the dominant eddic verse-form *fornyrðislag* ('old story metre'), while the mythological section, the first two stanzas and concluding encomium are in *ljóðaháttr*, 'song form'.

The following page, E5b, is blank.

[59]

INTRODUCTION.

" HACON, the subject of the fol-
" lowing piece, was son of the ce-
" lebrated Harold Harfax, whose death
" is recorded in Regner's ode. He was
" the great hero of the Norwegians,
" and the last of their Pagan kings.
" Hacon was slain about the year 960
" in a battle with the Danes, in which
" eight of his brethren fell before
" him. Eyvindur his cousin, a famous
" scald, or poet, who was present
" at the battle, composed this poem
" to be sung at his funeral.——What
" seems to have suggested the plan of
" the ode, was Hacon's surviving the
" battle, and afterwards dying of his
" wounds, which were not at first ap-
" prehended to be mortal. Although
                                    " this

1.

1. The first paragraph of Percy's Introduction up to the dash is almost word for word translated from the introductory paragraph to Mallet's translation of *Hákonarmál*, except that Percy substitutes 'Harold Harfax' for Mallet's *Harald aux beaux cheveux* and leaves out Mallet's explanation of Eyvindr's nickname *skáldaspillir*, which he says means '*la croix des Poétes* à cause de ses talens superieurs pour les vers'. Eyvindr was related to King Haraldr hárfagri on his mother's side.

[60]

" this is not very clear from the hif-
" tory, fomething of this kind muft be
" underftood, to render the poem in-
" telligible.

1.

" To fave the neceffity of many
" notes, we muft remind the Reader,
" that ODIN or WODEN was worfhip-
" ped in the northern nations, as the
" god of war, and as father of the
" other gods. Such as died in battle
" were believed to be received into the
" habitation of the gods, and there to
" feaft and carroufe full goblets of the
" northern nectar ALE and BEER; this
" place or Elizium was called *Valhall*
" or the hall of flaughter. To receive
" an invitation to *Valhall* or the palace
" of the gods meant the fame as to re-
" ceive a death-fummons.

" The

1. Percy's explanatory paragraph on the mythological background to the poem, 'to save the necessity of many notes', recalls Shenstone's advice to him in a letter of 1 October 1760 (see *Introduction, Thomas Percy as a Translator of Old Norse Poetry* for the text).

[61]

" The Islandic original of this poem
" is preferved in Snorro Sturlefon's *Hiſt.*
" *Regum Septentrionalium,* folio. vol. 1.
" pag. 163. The Latin verfion of Pe-
" ringſkiold has been chiefly followed,
" except in fome few places in which
" the preference was given to that of
" Bartholin in his *Cauſæ de contempt.*
" *a Danis mortis,* and to the French
" tranflation of the Chev. Mallet in his
" *L' Edda, pag.* 159."

THE

The following page, E7b, is blank.

[63]

THE

FUNERAL SONG

O F

H A C O N.

GONDUL and Scogul, the god-
deffes of deftiny, were fent by
Odin to chufe, among the kings, one
of the race of Yngvon, who fhould go
dwell with him in the palace of the
gods.

1.

They found the brother of Biorno
putting on his coat of mail: that excellent king ftood ready under the ban-
ner: the enemies fell; the fword was
brandifhed; the conflict was begun.

2.

The

1. Percy's explanatory 'the goddesses of destiny' is not in the Icelandic text, though Peringskiöld places *Parcas* in parentheses after the two valkyries' names. We have seen earlier how reluctant Percy seems to have been to use the Scandinavian-derived word 'valkyrie' in his translations. Peringskiöld gives 'Gothorum Mars' for the Icelandic Óðinn-name *Gautatýr*, and his notebook (f. 26r) shows that Percy was at one stage misled into thinking the name was a reference to Þórr. However, Bartholin's translation is clear on this point and Percy seems to have followed it. Percy also uses the erroneous form 'Yngvon' for 'Yngvi' in a stanza from *Háleygjatal*, also by Eyvindr (see *Translations from the works of Viking Age skalds* 1.2, note 3). Apparently unwilling to use the name Valhǫll in his translation, though he has cited it in his Introduction to *Hákonarmál*, Percy renders *[hverr] skyldi með Óðni fara/ í Valhǫll at vera*, 'who should go to be with Óðinn in Valhalla', by 'who should go dwell with him in the palace of the gods'. His notebook version (f. 26r) runs 'Who should go with Odin to inhabit Walhall' with the note to the latter, 'The Gothick Elizium'.

2. 'the brother of Biorno' is Hákon himself. Percy usually derives the nominative forms of Norse proper names from Peringskiöld's Latin translation, applying the rules of Latin, rather than Old Norse grammar to the process. Thus he deduces an erroneous form *Biorno from Peringskiöld's 'Fratrem Biornonis'. For Percy's translation of *darraðr* here as 'sword', see the note to his translation of this word in 'The Ransome of Egill the Scald'.

[64]

1.
The flayer of princes had conjured
the inhabitants of Haleyg: he had conjured the inhabitants of the ifles: he
went to the battle. The renowned
chief had a gallant retinue of northern
men. The depopulator of the Danifh
iflands ftood under his helmet.

2.
The leader of the people had juft
before caft afide his armour; he had
put off his coat of mail: he had thrown
them down in the field a little before
the beginning of the battle. He was
playing with the fons of renowned men,
when he was called forth to defend his
kingdom. The gallant king now ftood
under his golden helmet.

3.
Then the fword in the king's hand
cut the coverings of brafs, as eafily as
if

1. 'the inhabitants of Haleyg' are the people of Hálogaland, *Halogiæ incolas* in Peringskiöld's Latin version, while Percy's unspecific 'the inhabitants of the isles' stands for the Norse text's *Holmrygir*, 'the people of Rogaland', explained by Peringskiöld as 'Holmrygenses, (id est Rogalandenses insulanos)'.

2. Percy follows Peringskiöld's Latin aside from a few minor touches of his own. Thus Hákon becomes 'the gallant king' rather than *gramr enn glaðværi* of the Old Norse or the Latin *Hilaris ille Rex*. Apparently it was more becoming for an ancient Northern king to be gallant than joyful on the field of battle.

3. The Old Norse text here has *vǫðir Váfaðar*, 'clothes of Váfǫðr (or Vǫfuðr)' [Óðinn] [ARMOUR], which Peringskiöld's Latin renders *gladius ... ænea tegumenta secuit*.

[65]

if it had been brandiſhed in water.
The javelins claſhed together: the
ſhields were broken: the arms reſounded on the ſculls of men.

The arms of Tyr, the arms of Bauga * were broke to pieces; ſo hard
were the helmets of the northern warriors.   They joined battle in the iſland
Storda.   The kings broke through the
ſhining fences of ſhields: they ſtained
them with human blood.

The ſwords waxed hot † in the
wounds diſtilling blood.   The long

* Tyr and Bauga were two ſubordinate gods
of war: the expreſſion means no more than the
Martia tela of Virgil.

† Or perhaps more literally, "burnt in the
" wounds."   One name for ſwords among the
Runic poets is, " The fires of wounds," Latin
Vulnerum ignes.

F   ſhields

1. Percy, following Peringskiöld, misunderstands the first half of this stanza, turning *Bauga into a mythological figure and not comprehending that Týr belongs in a kenning, *bauga Týr*, 'Týr [god] of rings', [WARRIOR]. The rest of the half-stanza then becomes hard to construe, and, though Peringskiöld recognised a reference to skulls (*hausar*, line 4), he does not get the syntax right. Modern editors read *Trǫddusk tǫrgur/ fyr Týs ok bauga/ hjalta harðfótum/ hausar Norðmanna*, as 'Shields along with skulls were crushed by the hard legs of the hilts [SWORD BLADES] of the Týr [god] of rings [WARRIOR, viz. Hákon] and the Norwegians.'

   'in the island Storda': the text has *í eyju*, 'on the island', actual naming of it being deferred until the last line of the following stanza. Peringskiöld is even more precise and names the place, Fitjar, on the island of Storð, where Hákon was being entertained when news was brought that his enemies were at hand.

2. The text reads *Brunnu beneldar/ í blóðgum undum*, 'wound-fires [SWORDS] burnt in the bloody wounds'. Peringskiöld explained the kenning in a note to the Latin translation, 'Vulnerum ignes (id est gladii)'.

[66]

ſhields inclined themſelves over the
lives of men. The deluge from the ſpears
ran down the ſhore of Storda: there on
that promontory fell the wounded bodies.

1.

Wounds ſuffuſed with gore were received among the ſhields; while they
played in the battle contending for ſpoil.
The blood rapidly flowed in the ſtorm
of Odin. Many men periſhed thro'
the flowings from the ſword.

2.

Then fate the chiefs with their
blunted ſwords; with broken and ſhat-
tered ſhields; with their coats of mail
pierced thro' with arrows. The hoſt
no longer thought of viſiting the habitation of the gods.

3.

When lo! Gondul leaned on her
lance

3

1. Percy's 'long shields' follows a similar phrase in Peringskiöld's Latin, but the compound *langbarðar*, 'long beards' in line 3 probably refers to swords, not shields. 'The deluge from the spears ran down the shore of Storda: there on that promontory fell the wounded bodies' follows a suggestion in Peringskiöld's Latin that the kenning *sverða nes*, 'promontory of swords' [SHIELD] should be taken literally, *in gladiorum promontorio, (ubi pugna stetit)*.

   The second half-stanza is more likely to read *svarraði sárgymir/ á sverða nesi, / fell flóð fleina/ í fjǫru Storðar*, 'the wound-sea [BLOOD] roared on the headland of swords [SHIELD], a flood of shafts [BLOOD] fell on the shore of Storð'.

2. The first part of this stanza is not only difficult syntactically, but full of kennings, one battle-kenning, *Skǫglar veðr*, 'storms of Skǫgul', and two shield-kennings, *himinn randar*, 'heaven of the rim' and *ský bauga*, 'clouds of the bosses'. Peringskiöld understands this in part, but does not really see how the various word groups relate to one another, and Percy's version is even further from the meaning. In the second half-stanza Percy retains two kennings, 'the storm of Odin' [BATTLE] and 'the flowings from the sword' (*mækis straumr*) [BLOOD], but loses *umðu oddláar*, 'the spearpoint-waves [BLOOD] roared', and this becomes 'the blood rapidly flowed'. This was not signalled in Peringskiöld's Latin, whereas the first two kennings were.

3. It is not clear why Percy translated 'blunted swords', when the Old Norse has *með sverð of togin*, 'with drawn swords', and Peringskiöld translated *[Reges] ... gladiis cincti* reading *umtoginn*. Percy may have missed the point of the last three lines *Vara sá herr/ í hugum ok átti/til Valhallar vega*, 'that army was not in a cheerful mood yet had to make its way to Valhalla', though Peringskiöld understood it, *Ille exercitus non in animo habuit Walhallam versus iter facere*. However, his exclamatory and contrastive 'When lo!' at the beginning of the following stanza suggests a willful alteration. The exclamation has no counterpart in either the Norse text or in Peringskiöld.

[67]

lance and thus befpake them, The affembly of the gods is going to be increafed, for they invite Hacon with a mighty hoft to their banquet.

The king heard what the beautiful nymphs of war, fitting on their horfes, fpake. The nymphs feemed full of thought: they were covered with their helmets: they had their fheilds before them.

Hacon faid, Why haft thou, O goddefs, thus difpofed of the battle? Were we not worthy to have obtained a more perfect victory?——Thou oweft to us, retorted Scogul, that thou haft carried the field: that thy enemies have betaken themfelves to flight.

F 2   Scogul

1. The last line of Peringskiöld's text reads *heimbauþ umboþit*, 'ad convivium invitarunt', rather than *heim bǫnd of boðit*, 'the gods [have] invited [Hákon] home', which is the reading adopted by many modern editors.

2. Once again, Percy refrains from calling a valkyrie a valkyrie, instead producing 'the beautiful nymphs of war', doubtless encouraged by Peringskiöld's *elegantes bellorum Nymphæ* for *valkyrjur ... mærar*, 'the glorious (or, famous) valkyries'.

[68]

Scogul the wealthy * fpake thus;
Now we muft ride through the green
worlds of the gods, to tell Odin that
the all-powerful king is coming to his
hall; that he is coming to vifit him.

1.

The father of the gods faid, Her-
mode and Brago, my fons, go to meet
the king: for now Hacon, the admired
warrior, approacheth to our hall.

2.

The king was now arrived from the
battle, he ftood all befprinkled with
blood and faid; Odin appeareth very
fevere and terrible: he fmileth not upon
my foul.

3.

* The DESTINIES are called rich or wealthy,
becaufe they finally inherit and poffefs all things.

Brago

1. 'The father of the gods' is Percy's periphrasis for the stanza's *Hroptatýr*, one of the names of Óðinn, while the explanatory 'my sons', which is not in the Old Norse text, was suggested by Peringskiöld's *Hermodus & Brago (mei filii)*. Hermóðr was one of Óðinn's sons in Norse mythology, but Bragi was not. Hákon is not mentioned by name in this stanza, the noun *konungr*, 'king', being used instead.

2. Percy's rather effective conclusion to this verse is suggested by Peringskiöld's *ille nostro animo non arridet*. Most manuscripts have *séum vér um hans hugi*, 'We are [=I am] afraid of his disposition', not reading *hann* with Peringskiöld's text.

3. The epithet (*en ríkja Skǫgul*) that Percy, following Peringskiöld, translates as 'wealthy' (*dives illa Scogula*), is more likely to mean 'mighty, powerful' in this context.

180

[69]

Brago faid, Thou fhall have peace here with all the heroes: drink ALE therefore with the gods. Thou deftroyer of princes haft here within eight brethren.

The good king anfwered; We will retain our arms*: the mail and helmet are carefully to be retained: it is good to have the fword in readinefs.

Then was feen how religioufly the king had performed all facred duties; fince the great council of the gods, and all the leffer divinities received Hacon among them with acclamations of welcome.

* Meaning that he would only enjoy warlike amufements, for fo they believed their heroes were employed in Elyfium.————It is probably a poetical infinuation that he would have his arms buried with him.

F 3   That

1. This clause translates *hvé sá konungr hafði/ vel of þyrmt véum*, 'how the king had dealt most reverently with the sanctuaries', referring to Hákon's role as the protector of pagan sanctuaries, in contrast to the example of his successor Haraldr greycloak, whose mistreatment of his people and his land are condemned in the poem's final stanza.

2. Percy's interpretation of this verse is far from the general view of modern scholars, who see Eyvindr's representation of Hákon's wary and distrustful attitude to Valhalla as indicative of a general scepticism towards the pagan religion.

[70]

1. That king is born on a fortunate day, who gains to himfelf fuch favour from the gods. The age in which he hath lived fhall ever be held in high remembrance.

2. The wolf Fenris *, freed from his chains, fhall range through the world among the fons of men, before fo re-nowned and fo good a king fhall again tread the defolate path of his kingdom.

3. Riches perifh : relations die : king-doms are laid wafte. Let Hacon dwell with the magnificent gods: While many nations are plunged in grief.

* By the wolf Fenris, the northern nations un-derftood a kind of demon or evil principle at en-mity with the gods, who, tho' at prefent chained up from doing mifchief, was hereafter to break loofe and deftroy the world. See the Edda.

THE

1. Percy's translation, doubtless influenced by Peringskiöld's Latin *qui talem famam sibi acquirit*, alters the Old Norse *er sér getr slíkan sefa*, 'who gains for himself such a temperament', by suggesting that Hákon's success is gained by divine favour, whereas the text puts the emphasis on his innate virtues.

2. There are some inaccuracies in the translation of this verse, introduced by Peringskiöld and followed by Percy. The Old Norse text has *á yta sjǫt*, 'on the homes of men', not 'the sons of men' as Percy has it and the last clause means 'before so good a prince should succeed to his vacant place'.

3. The first two lines of this stanza echo *Hávamál* 76-7, which contrast the mortality of humans and their possessions with the undying power of fame. Here there is no such expression of confidence; instead, the narrating voice dwells gloomily on the hard fate of Hákon's country and people after his death.

   Percy's translation of this stanza seems to owe more to Bartholin's Latin version than to Peringskiöld's, for he chooses 'riches' for *fé* in the first line (Bartholin has *divitiæ*, Peringskiöld *pecudes*), and he gives 'kingdoms are laid waste' (Bartholin has *vastatur terra*, while Peringskiöld chooses *regio & tota terra desolatur* for *eyðisk land ok láð*, 'land and country are laid waste'). His translation of the last part of the stanza resembles Bartholin's rather than Peringskiöld's, the former using a manuscript that read *siti Hakon/ med heidin god/ morg er þiod of þiad*, rather than *sízt* ... 'since ...'. Bartholin translates this as *maneat Haqvinus apud munificos Deos: dolet hominum multiudo*, which is close to the sense of Percy's translation, whereas Peringskjöld has *posteaquam Haco (Adalstenii Alumnus) ad Ethnicorum Deos commigravit, multæ nationes allictæ sunt*. The latter is closer to most modern editors' preferences.

(V.)

THE

COMPLAINT

OF

HAROLD.

F 4

'The Complaint of Harold' is the title Percy gave to a collection of six out of a supposed sixteen *gamanvísur*, 'pleasurable verses, humorous verses', as Snorri Sturluson terms them in *Haralds saga Sigurðarsonar* in *Heimskringla*, where only one (the first in Percy's version) is cited in Chapter 15 (Bjarni Aðalbjarnarson III, 1951, 88-9). Five additional verses, which may originally have belonged to a longer poem, are cited in the compilation *Morkinskinna* (Andersson and Gade 2000, 148-9), in *Fagrskinna* and *Hulda-Hrokkinskinna* (for a text of the six verses see Finnur Jónsson 1912-15 A I, 357-9 and B I, 329-30). According to Snorri, the Norwegian king Haraldr Sigurðarson harðráði ('the hard ruler') composed a poem of sixteen verses, each with the same concluding lines, on his way to Kiev from the Black Sea. Haraldr, who reigned from 1046-66, was noted as a poet as well as a Viking adventurer and ruler (cf. Turville-Petre 1968). The stanzas are in the skaldic measure *dróttkvætt*.

Percy was the first to translate these verses into English. His sources, as he indicates in his Introduction to the poem, were Bartholin (1689, 154-7) and Mallet (1756, 156-8, *Ode de Harald le vaillant*). Apart from a single short note on f.1r of Bodley MS Percy c. 7 (for the text see Clunies Ross 1998, 88), there is no material relating to 'The Complaint of Harold' in Percy's Bodleian notebook. However, a transcript of the Icelandic text and Latin translation from Bartholin exists now as National Library of Wales, Panton MS 74, f. 109a-c. This transcript originally accompanied a letter of 25 July 1762 that Percy sent to his Welsh correspondent Evan Evans (see *A chronology of Percy's translations* and Clunies Ross 1998, 88 for the details). As Percy did not receive a copy of Bartholin until 26 March 1762, it is likely that his work on 'The Complaint of Harold' took place after that date, and it may have been the last of the translations in *Five Pieces* to have been undertaken. 'The Complaint of Harold' is Smith 1989 PeT 21, but has no separate siglum, PeT 21 standing for Bodley MS Percy c. 7 as a whole. It is Clunies Ross 1998, 88, no. 5.

For Mallet, whose sentiments Percy in part reflects in his Introduction, this poem was proof that the ancient Scandinavians could compose on the subject of 'the softer passions', and not be 'altogether taken up with blood and death and other images of horror'. Even in his first edition, however, Mallet took a stronger line, which Percy was later to endorse more firmly in *Northern Antiquities*. In the short introduction to his own translation of the poem, Mallet presents the ancient Scandinavians and other Germanic peoples as the true originators of romantic love and romantic poetry. For him Haraldr's verses are enough to show that 'les Peuples du Nord ont imaginé d'associer l'amour & la valeur guerriére avant les nations mêmes dont ils ont eu ensuite

le plus de penchant à adopter tous les goûts. ...Dans cette Ode il se plaint de ce que la gloire qu'il s'étoit acquise par tant d'exploits n'avoit pû toucher Elissif fille de Jarislas Roi de Russie.'

The following page, F4b, is blank.

[73]

INTRODUCTION.

" HAROLD, furnamed The Va-
" liant, lived about the mid-
" dle of the eleventh century, and was
" one of the moſt illuſtrious adventu-
" rers of his time. Piracy was con-
" ſidered among the northern nations,
" as the only road to riches and glory:
" in purſuit of theſe Harold had not
" only run thro' all the northern ſeas,
" but had even penetrated into the Me-
" diterranean, and made many ſucceſs-
" ful attempts on the coaſts of Africa
" and Sicily. He was at length taken
" priſoner and detained for ſome time
" at Conſtantinople. In this ode he
" complains that all the glory he had
" ac-

[74]

" acquired by fo many exploits had not
" been able to move the heart of Eli-
" zabeth daughter of Jariflaus king of
" Ruffia.

" The following piece is only a frag-
" ment; for the ode originally confift-
" ed of fixteen ftanzas: it is alfo much
" more modern than any of the former.
" It was notwithftanding acceptable,
" as the fubject of it turns upon the
" fofter paffions, and is not altogether
" taken up with blood and death and
" other images of horror, like the reft.

" The original of this fragment is
" printed in Bartholin's excellent trea-
" tife intitled, *Caufæ contemptæ a Da-*
" *nis mortis,* 4to 1689. *p.* 54: where it
" is accompanied with a literal Latin
                                    " ver-

1. The first two paragraphs of Percy's Introduction follow Mallet's very closely, but with less emphasis on the importance of the poem as evidence of the ancient Scandinavians' pioneering of the phenomenon of courtly love.
2. The correct page reference is 154 (154-7), as Percy indicates at the beginning of 'The Islandic Original of the Complaint of Harold' on p. 98 of *Five Pieces*.

[75]

" verfion, which we have chiefly fol-
" lowed, except in one or two paffa-
" ges, where the preference feemed
" due to the French tranflation of the
" Chevalier Mallet, publifhed in his
" *L' Edda*, 4*to* 1755. Bartholin tells
" us he had the original out of an old
" Islandic hiftory, intitled *Knitlinga*
" *Saga*."

THE

The following page, F6b, is blank.

[77]

THE

COMPLAINT

OF

HAROLD.

MY ship hath sailed round the isle
of Sicily. Then were we all
magnificent and splendid. My brown
vessel, full of warriors, rapidly skimmed
along the waves. Eager for the fight,
I thought my sails would never slacken:
1.   And yet a Russian maid disdains me.

I fought in my youth with the inhabitants of Drontheim. They had troops
superior in number. Dreadful was the
conflict. Young, as I was, I left their
young

1. Percy's translation here, based loosely on Bartholin, gives the general sense of the verse but little of the detail. The first line should read 'The ship cut past broad Sicily'. Bartholin's text and translation produces a number of variations from interpretations accepted by most modern editors, including 'my brown vessel' and 'Eager for the fight, I thought my sails would never slacken', the last of which is normally interpreted to mean that the ship went so fast that no laggard could catch up with it.

   The last two lines of the verse, which Percy translates as 'And yet a Russian maid disdains me', form the iterated conclusion to all verses according to Bartholin, Mallet and Percy, but are in fact lacking in the fourth verse, where Haraldr lists all his accomplishments. The Icelandic text has *Þó lætr Gerðr í Gǫrðum/ gollhrings við mér skolla*, 'Yet the Gerðr [giantess] of the gold ring [WOMAN] in Garðar holds herself aloof from me'. Garðar or Garðaríki was the name given in Old Norse texts to the lands east of the Baltic. Although the reference in this refrain-like sequence is non-specific, Bartholin, following his Old Norse sources, interprets it to allude to Ellisif, daughter of Prince Jarizleifr (Jaroslav) of Kiev, whom Haraldr married shortly after this journey according to Old Icelandic sources.

[78]

1. young king dead in the fight. And yet
a Ruffian maid difdains me.

2. One day we were but fixteen on
fhip-board : a tempeft rofe and fwelled
the ocean. The waves filled the loaded veffel: but we diligently cleared it.
Thence I formed the brighteft hopes.
And yet a Ruffian maid difdains me.

3. I know how to perform eight exercifes. I fight with courage. I keep a
firm feat on horfeback. I am fkilled
in fwimming. I glide along the ice
on fcates. I excell in darting the lance.
I am dextrous at the oar. And yet
a Ruffian maid difdains me.

What tender maid or widow can deny, that in the morning, when, pofted
near

1. If this collection of stanzas reviews high points of Haraldr's life, in a way similar to *Krákumál*'s celebration of the life of Ragnarr loðbrók, then the present stanza should come at the beginning, for it refers to Haraldr's fighting at the age of fifteen alongside his half-brother King Óláfr Haraldsson at the battle of Stiklastaðir in 1030. After the king's death, Haraldr went into exile in Garðar and spent the next fifteen years in the service of Jaroslav of Kiev.

2. The first four lines of this verse are attributed to the Icelandic chieftain Njáll Þórgeirsson (d. 1011) rather than to Haraldr harðráði in manuscripts of Snorri Sturluson's *Edda* (Faulkes 1998 I, 215) but to Haraldr in *Morkinskinna* and *Hulda*. No other verse is attributed to Njáll (for the Icelandic text, see Andersson and Gade 2000, 148 and Finnur Jónsson 1912-15 A I, 138-9 and B I, 130). The stanza, which contains a stereotypical address to an unspecified woman (*svanni*), seems to describe a sudden storm at sea and the efforts of the crew of sixteen to bale out the boat from four stations. Percy's '*One day* we were *but* sixteen ...' (my italics) seeks to dramatise the situation and here follows Mallet's translation rather than Bartholin's. The Icelandic text of the second half of the stanza is the same as the second half of stanza 1, though one would never realise it from Percy's or Mallet's translations.

3. This verse, as Percy himself recognised, and discusses in his Postscript on pages 80-82 of *Five Pieces*, is very similar to one ascribed in Chapter 58 of *Orkneyinga saga* to the Orkney earl Rǫgnvaldr kali Kolsson (d. 1158), which Percy knew both from Ole Worm's Appendix to *Literatura Runica* and from Bartholin. Lines 5-8 of the stanzas ascribed to the two poets are the same, while lines 1-4 show differences in the accomplishments enumerated.

   Percy, following Bartholin and Mallet, makes Haraldr claim as his first accomplishment that 'I fight with courage'. However, the Icelandic text gives the first skill as the composition of poetry, *Yggs fetk líð at smíða*, 'I know how to create Yggr's [=Óðinn] drink [POETRY]'. The qualifying *stundum*, 'sometimes', though reflected in Bartholin's version, is missing from Percy's and Mallet's 'I am skilled in swimming', a closer translation being 'I have sometimes taken to swimming'. This may, of course, be an understatement. The last two accomplishments, of playing the harp and composing poetry, are suppressed in the version of this stanza Bartholin cites in favour of the refrain-like reference to the 'Gerðr of the gold ring' and her continuing disdain of Haraldr.

[79]

near the city in the fouth, we joined
battle; can deny that I bravely wielded
my arms; or that I left behind me laft-
ing monuments of my valour. And

1.   yet a Ruffian maid difdains me.

I was born in the uplands of Norway, where the inhabitants handle fo
well the bow. Now I make my fhips,
the dread of peafants, rufh among the
rocks of the fea. Far from the abode
of men, I have plowed the wide ocean
with my veffels. And yet a Ruffian

2.   maid difdains me.

POSTSCRIPT.

1. Percy's version of this stanza is closer to Mallet's than to Bartholin's. The point of the first section is that if women had been watching Haraldr when, one morning, he was fighting in an unspecified town, they would have seen him get down to work early. On the conventional skaldic topos of women watching men fight or engage in other deeds of prowess, see Frank 1990 and Fidjestøl 1997.

2. The translation of this final stanza of 'The Complaint of Harold' owes something to both Bartholin and Mallet. The first sentence is a word-for-word translation of Mallet's French 'Je suis né dans le haut païs de Norvége, là où les habitans manient si bien les arcs'.

[80]

P O S T - S C R I P T.

" In the preceding poem Harold
" mentions EIGHT exercifes, but enu-
1. " merates only FIVE. If the Reader
" is inquifitive to know what thofe are,
" which he has omitted, he may col-
" lect them from the following ancient
" Runic verfes. Wherein a northern
" hero is introduced boafting of him-
" felf,

2.   *Tafl em ek aurr at* &c.

" I am mafter of nine accomplifh-
3. ments. I play well at chefs. I know
how to engrave Runic letters. I am
apt at my book; and know how to
handle the tools of the fmith. I tra-
verfe

1. Six skills, not five, are enumerated in the verse Percy gives, fighting, horse riding, swimming, skating (or skiing), throwing the lance and rowing.

2. This is the verse ascribed to Rǫgnvaldr kali Kolsson, Jarl of the Orkneys, mentioned in the note to the fourth stanza of 'The Complaint of Harold'. Percy knew a runic version of this verse in Ole Worm's *Literatura Runica* (1636, 129) and an Icelandic text and Latin translation in Bartholin (1689, 420-1). He sent a transcript of the text from Bartholin to Evan Evans, enclosed with the same letter in which he sent him 'The Complaint of Harold'. The transcript is now National Library of Wales, Panton MS 74, f. 109d. This verse is not listed by Smith 1989, but it is Clunies Ross 1998, 89, no. 7. The 'Islandic Original' is on p. 99 of *Five Pieces*.

3. Bartholin has *ludum scachicum* here. The Old Norse word is *tafl*, L. *tabula*, 'tables', a board game played through much of early Northern Europe and similar to the game known in English as Fox and Geese.

[81]

verfe the fnow on fcates of wood. I
excell in fhooting with the bow; and
in managing the oar. I fing to the
harp; and compofe verfes."

Olj. Wormij. Lit. Run. pag. 129.——
Barthol. Caufæ &c. pag. 420.

" We fhall conclude this fubject,
" with a celebrated character from
" the ancient chronicles of Norway.
" viz."

"King Olaf Tryggefon was ftronger,
more alert and nimble than any man of
his time. He would climb the rock
Smalferhorn, and fix his fhield on the
top of it. He would walk without
the boat on the oars while the men
were rowing. He would play with

G   three

[82]

three darts at once ; toffing them up in
the air, and always keeping two up,
while one was down in his hand. He
was ambi-dexter, and could ufe his
weapon with both hands, and throw
two javelins at once. He excelled all
his men in fhooting with the bow:
And in fwimming he had no equal."

1.

See Pontoppidan's Hift. of Norway,
pag. 248.

THE END.

1. Percy received a copy of this book from Dodsley in London some time after 6 May 1761, according to Bodleian MS Percy c. 9, f. 96v.

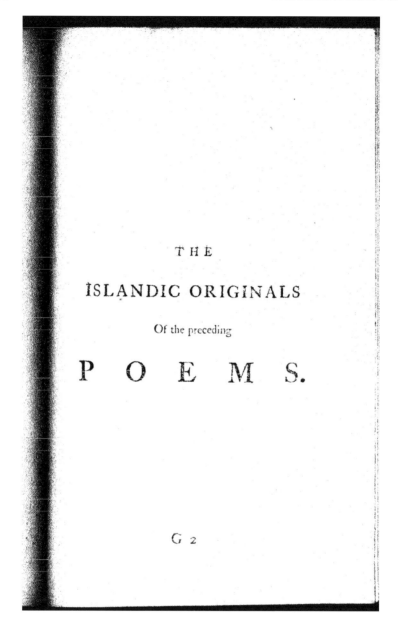

THE

ÎSLANDIC ORIGINALS

Of the preceding

P O E M S.

G 2

Comments on Percy's use and understanding of his various source texts are distributed throughout the notes to his translations. His transcriptions are reasonably accurate, though the degree of accuracy varies from poem to poem. Given that he had to transcribe the texts of 'The Dying Ode of Regner Lodbrog' and 'The Ransome of Egill the Scald' from Ole Worm's runic versions, he has done a commendable job, though there are a fair number of errors, especially in the latter poem. Some transcription errors have been mentioned in the notes. The Old Norse texts that Percy used and reproduced are invariably in the modernised Icelandic form which was universal in seventeenth- and eighteenth-century editions.

[85]

I.

THE ISLANDIC ORIGINAL

OF THE

INCANTATION OF HERVOR.

V. Hervarer Saga, Olaj Verelj. Upfal. 1672. fol. p. 91.

HERVOR.

*V*Akadnu Angantyr,
    Vekur thig Hervor
Einka dotter
Yckar Suafu :
Sel thu mer ur hauge
Hardan mækir,
Than er Suafurlama
Slogu duergar.

Hervardur, Hiorvardur,
Hrani oc Angantyr,
Vek eg ijdr alla
Vidar under rotum,
Med hialmi oc briniu,
Oc huoffa fuerdi,
Raund oc reida,
Oc rodaun geiri.

Ero miog vordner
Andgryms fyner
Mein-giarner ad
Molldar auka !
Ad eingi gior fona
Eyvor vid mig mæla
Ur munar heimi !
Hervardur, Horvardur.

Suo fie ijdur aullum
Innan rifia
Sem er i maura
Mornid hangi,
Nema fuerd felier,
Thad er flogu duergar
Samyra draugum ;
Dyrt um fetla.

[I thui hili opnuduſt hau-
gar, oc var alt ad fia fem
logi eirn, oc tha var thetta
quedid i hauge Angantyrs :]

ANGANTYR.
Hervor dotter
Huij kallar fuo,
Full feikiuftafa,
Fer thu ad illu ?
Od ertu ordin
Oc orvita
Vill-higgiandi
Vekia dauda menn.

Grofu mig ey fader
Nie frændur adrer.
Their haufdu Tirfing

G 3   *Tueir*

[86]

Tueir er lifdu,
Vard tho eigandi
Einn af sijdan.

HERVOR.
Satt mæir thu ecki.
So lati As tilig
Heilan i haugi
Sem thu hofir eigi
Tirfing med thier.
Trautter thier ad veita
Arf Angantyr
Einka barne.

ANGANTYR.
Seige eg thier, Hervor
Thad vera mun,
Sa mun Tirfingur
(Ef thu trua mætter)
Ætt thinni nær
Allre spilia.
Muntu son gieta,
Thann sijdar mun
Tirfing hafa,
Oc trua marger
Hann munu Heidrek
Heita lyder.

HERVOR.
Eg of-kingi
So virda dauda
Ad thier tholed
Alldrey kyrrer,
Nema Angantyr
Selier mier Tirfing,
Hlyfum heittan,
Hialmars bana.

ANGANTYR.
Mær qued eg unga

Monnum lijka,
Er um hauga
Huarlar à nottuns,
Grofnum geiri
Med gotta malum,
Hialm oc briniu
Fyre hallar dyr.

HERVOR.
Madur thotter thu
Menskur tilforna
Adur eg sali
Ydra tok kanna :
Sel thu mier ur haugi
Than er hatar brinju
Duerga smidis
Duger thier ey ad leina.

ANGANTYR.
Liggur mier under herdum
Hialmars bani,
Allur er han utan
Elldi sueipinn.
Mey veit eg aungva
Molld à huorge
Er than hior thori
Hond i nema.

HERVOR.
Eg mun hirda
Oc i haund nema
Huassan mæki
Ef eg hafa gnædi.
Hygg eg eige
Ella brenna than
Er framlidnum firdum
Leikur uin sioner.

ANGANTYR.
Heimsk ertu Hervor

[87]

Hugar eigandi,
Er thu ad augum
I elld hrapar,
Helldur vil eg fuerd thier
Selia ur haugi,
Mær en unga,
Mun eg thig ey leina.

[*Tha var fuerd i hendi*
Hervarar, oc quad hon:]

HERVOR.
Vel giorder thu
Vikings nidur
Er thu fender mier
Suerd ur haugi :
Betur thikiumft nu
Budlungur hafa
Enn eg Noreyge
Næde allre.

ANGANTYR.
Veiftu ey ad
Uppfol ertu
Mala, fiarad kona
Thui thu fagna fkalt.
Sa mun Tirfingur
(Ef thu trua nædur.)
Ætt thinni mær
Allri fpilla.

HERVOR.
Eg mun ganga
Til gialfur-manna;
Hier mun ey mær
I hug godum.
Litt ræke eg thad
Lofdunga vinur
Huad fyner miner
Sijdan deile.

ANGANTYR.
Thu fkalt eiga
Oc unna leingi ;
Hafdu ad huldu
Hialmars bana,
Taktu ad eggium,
Eitur er i badum,
Sæ er mans matadur
Miklum verri.

HERVOR.
Eg mun hirda
Oc i haund nema
Huaffan mæki ·
Er mig hafa latid :
Ugge eg eye thad,
Ulfa greinir,
Huad fyner miner
Sijdan telia.

ANGANTYR.
Far vil dotter,
Fliott gief eg thièr
Tolf manna fior,
Ef thu trua nædir,
Afl oc eliom,
Alt hid goda
Er fyner Angryms
Epter leifdu.

HERVOR.
Bui thier aller,
Burt mun eg fkiotla,
Heiler i hauge,
Hiedan fyfer mig.
Helft thottunft eg
Heima i mille
Er mig umhuerfis
Elldar brunnu.

G 4   II. THE

[88]

II.

THE ISLANDIC ORIGINAL,

OF THE

DYING ODE OF REGNER LODBROG,

V. Literatur. Runic. Olaj Wormij. Hafniæ 1636.
4to. p. 197.

BIARKAMAL
SEM ORTE REGNAR LODBROG.

*H*luggum vier med hiorve
  Hitt var æi fyrer longu
Er a Gautlande geinkum
At graf vitins morde
Tha feinkum vier Thoru
Thadan heitu mig firdar
Er lingaulum lagdag
Lodbrok ad thui vige
Stak eg a ftorear lykin
Stale biartra mala.

Hiuggum vier med hiorve
Helldur var ek ungur er
  feingum
Auftur i Eirar Sunde
Undarm frekum varge
Og fatgulum fugle
Fengum vier thar er fungu
Vid hafeymda hialma
Hard iarn mikils verdar
Allur var ægar folliam
Od rafa i valblode.

Hiuggum vier med hiorve

Hatt barum tha geira
Er tuituger toldunft
Og tyr rudum vyda
Uunnum atta Jarla
Auftur fyrer Thinu minne
Kera feigum tha gnoka
Gifting ad thui vike
Sueiti fiell i follium
Sae tynde lid aefe.

Hiuggum vier med hiorve
Hiedins kuonar vard andit
Tha er Helfinkin heimtum
Til heimfala Odins
Lokdum uppi ivu
Oddur naade tha byta
All var undo gialfre
Afaer vodin heitu
Greniade brandur i brynu
Beufilldur klufu fkylldi.

Hiuggum vier med hiorve
Hygg ek onguan tha flyde
Adur a hemlis heftum

[89]

Heraudur i ftyr fielle
Klyfur ei aegis aundrum
Allur Jarlin faegre
Lunda voll til loegis
A langfkipum fydan
Sa bar fiklungur vida
Snart fram i ftyr hiarta.

Hiuggum vier med hiorve
Her kaftade fkialldum
Tha er hraegagare ronde
Reiftur ad gunna brieftum
Beit i Skarfua fkerium
Shaeribildur at hialdri
Rodinn var randar mane
Adur Rafn kongur fielle
Dreif ur holda haufum
Heitum a brynniur fueite.

Hiuggum vier med hiorve
Haft getu tha rafnar
Fyrir In yndiris eiun
Axrna braad ad fyta
Fengum falu keftum
Fullann verd ad finne
Illt var eins ad geta
I uppruna folar
Strenghaumlur fa eg flinga
Stak almur af fier maalme.

Hiuggum vier med hiorve
Hett greniuda brottar
Adur a Ullar akre
Eifteinn kongur fielle
Gingum gulli faedur
Grandur vals ad braundum
Hraekindil fneid randa
Ritur ad hialma mote
Snira virtur ur farum
Sueif of fiarna kleifa.

Hiuggum vier med hiorve
Hofdum rendur i blode
Tha er benthuera braeddum
Fyrer Borgundar holme
Reggfky flitu rander
Ratt almur af fier malme
Volnir fiell at vige
Var at aei kongur meire
Val rak vitt um ftrandir
Vargur fagnade tafne.

Hiuggum vier med hiorve
Hilldur var fynt i vehfte
Adur Freyr kongur fille
A Flemingia lande
Nade blaer ad byta
Blode fmelttur i gyltann
Hogna-kufl ad hialldre
Hardur hengrefill fordum
Maer griet morgin fkaeru
Morg en tafn gafft vorgum.

Hiuggum vier med hiorve
Hundrudum fa eg liggia
A eireis aundrum
Thar Aeinglanes heitir
Sigldum vier til fnaeru
Sehs daegur adur lid fielle
Allum edda miffu
Fyrir upruna folar
Vard fyrir vorum fuerdum
Valdiofur i ftyr hniga.

Hiuggum vier med hiorve
Hrunde dogg af fuerdum
Eryn i Bardla yrde
Bleikon na fyrir hauka
Umde almur thar oddar
Aliftrit bitu fkyrtur
Ad flidur loga fennu

[90]

Suolnis hotte thaefdar
Rende almur til unda
Eiturhuas drifium fueita.

Hiuggum vier med hiorve
Hielldum klakar tiolldum
Hatt ad hildur leike
Fyrir Hiadninga-vage
Sia maittu tha feggir
Er fuerd rifu fkioldu
At bracfilldur bialldre
Hialm flitnad aun gotna
Vara: fem biarta brude
I bing bia fier leggia.

Hiuggum vier med hiorve
Herd kom brid a fkioldum
Naer fiell nidur til iardar
A Nordhumra-lande
Varat un eina ottu
Olldum thorf at flya
Hilldar leik thar er huaffer
Hialm-tun bitu fkiomar
Varat fem unga ekkiu
I ondueige kyffa.

Hiuggum vier med hiorve
Herthiofe vard audit
I futbur-einum fialftun
Sigurs a varum monnum
Vard i rauda regne
Raugnvalldur firir bniga
Sa kom haeftur yfur hauka
Harmur ad fuerda leike
Huaft kaftade brifter
Hialms ftrenglaugar palme.

Hiuggum vier med hiorve
Haer la thuer um anan
Gladur vard geira brydur

Gaukur at fuerda leike
Liet ei aurn nie ylge
Sa er Irlande ftyrde
Mot vard malms og ritar
Marftan kongur fafta
Vard i Vedra-firde
Valtafn gefit brafne.

Hiuggum vier med biorve
Her margan fa eg falla
Morgenftund fyrir maeker
Mann i odda fenniu
Syne minum bncit fnemma
Slidra tharn vid hiarta
Eigill liet Agnar raentann
Ohlaudann hal lyfe
Glunde geyr vid Hamdes
Grann ferk bliku merke.

Hiuggum vier med hiorvt
Halldarda fa eg prytia
Eke fmatt fyrir ulfa
Endils nidar brandum
Varat a vikar fkeide
Sem vinkonur baere
Hrodin var aegis afne
Ofar i dyn geyra
Skarin var fkoglar-kapa
Att Skioldunga bialldre.

Hiuggum vier med biorve
Harfagrann fa eg rankua
Meiar dreng enn um morgum
Og malvin ekkiu
Varat fem uormar laugur
Vinkiors niorun baere
Os i Ilafunde
Adur Auru kongur fielle
Blud mana fa eg brefta
Bra thad fira life.

[9¹]

Hiuggum vier med hiorve
Hadum fuerds ad morde
Leik a Lindis eire
Vid lofdunga threinna
Faer nade thui fakna
Fiell margur i gynvarge
Haukur fteit holld med ulfe
Ad hann heill thadann kuae-
    mift
Ira blod i aege
Aerit fiell um fkiru.

Hiuggum vier med hiorve
Ha fuerd bitu fkialldum
Tha er gullrodin glumde
Geir nid hildar naefre
Sia man i Onlugs eiu
Um alldur mega fydan
Thar er at logdis leike
Lofdungar fram-geingu
Rodinn var ut fyrir eire
Ar flugdreke fara.

Hiuggum vier med hiorve
Huad er drengur ad feigre
Ad hun i odda ele
Ondardur latinn uerdi
Oft fyter fa arfe
Er alldrege nefter
Illt kueda arg ann eggia
Auru ad fuerda leike
Hugblaudum keimur huorge
Hiarte fit ad gagne.

Hiuggum vier med hiorve
Hit tel eg iafnt ad gange
At famtoger fuerda
Sueinn i mote einum
Hrokkve ei thegn fyrir
    thegne

Thad var drengs adal leinge
Ae fkal aftuinur meia
Einardur i dyn fuerda.

Hiuggum vier med hiorve
Hitt fiunift mier raunar
At forlogom fylgium
Faar geingur um fkop narva
Aige hugdak Ellu
At aldur-lage minu
Tha er eg blod vale braedda
Og bord a log keirdag
Vitt fengum tha varge
Verd i Skotlands fiordum.

Hiuggum vier med hiorve
Hit blaeger mig iafnam
Thad Balldur fadur bekke
Buna veit eg at fumlum
Drekum BIOR ad bragde
Ur piukvidum haufa
Syter ei drengur vid dauda
Dyrs ad Fiolins hufum
Ei kem ek med eidru
Ord till Vidris hallar.

Hiuggum vier med hiorve
Hier uilldu nu aller
Burer Aflaugar brandum
Bitrum hillde vekkia
Ef vandlige viffe
Um vidfarar offar
Hue o-faer ormar
Eitur follir mig flyta
Madernis fek eg minum
Maugum fuo at hiartun
    duga.

Hiuggum vier med hiorve
Harda lidur at arfue

[92]

Grimt flendur grand af
    nodru
Geinn biggur fal hiarta
Vaentum hins ad Vidris
Vandur i Ella lblde
Sonum minum mune fuella
Sin moder rodinn verda
Ei munu fnarper faeinar
Sett kyrt vera lata.

  Huggun vier med hiorve
Hef eg fimtigum finna
Folk orvftur framdar
Fleindings bode og eina
Minft hugde eg manna

At mier vera fkyllde
Ungur nam eg odd at rioda
Annar kongur fremre
Os munu Acfar bioda
Er ei fytande daude.

  Fyfumft hins at haetta
Heimbiode mier Dyfir
Sem fra Herians hallu
Hefur Odinn mier fendar
Gladur fkaieg OL *med Afum*
I ondvege dreka
Lifs eru liduar flunder
Laegiande fkal eg deia.

III.

THE ISLANDIC ORIGINAL

OF THE

RANSOME OF EGILL THE SCALD.

V. Literatur. Runic. Olaj Wormij Hafniæ 1636.
4to. p. 227.

HOFUDLAUSTI
EGILS SCALLAGRYMS SONAR ISLANDSK KAPPA.

I. Vilfa.

Veftur kom eg um ver
    Enn eg Vidris ber
Manftrinder mar
Sa er mitt offer
Dro eg cik a flot
Vid Ijabrot
Hlod eg maerdar liit
Minis haarvar fkut.

II.

Bydunft hilmer blod
Nu a eg brodrar qued
Ber eg Odins miod
A Eingla beod
Lof at viifa vann
Vyft maere eg davn
Hliods bidium hann
Duiat brodur of fann.

[93]

III.
Hygg viiſer at
Vel ſomer that
Hue eg thylia fat
Ef eg thogn of-gat
Fleſtur madur of-fra
Huad fylker va
Enn vidrer ſa
Huar valur um la.

IV.
Ox biorva blom
Vid blyfar drom
Gudur vox um gram
Gramur ſogte fram
Thar beirdiſt tha
Thaut mackirs a
Malmbrydar ſpa
Su er meſt of-la.

V.
Var at villuſtadar
Veſur daradar
Of grams gladar
Geir vangs radar
Thars i blode
I brimla mode
Flauſter of drunde
Und um glumde

I. Stef.
Hnie firda ſit
Vid ſteinabnit
Ordſtyr of-gat
Eirikur at that

Nu hefir annat Stafiamal.
I.
Fremur mun eg ſeigia

Ef firdar theikia
Fragum fleira
Til frama theira
Aiſtuſt under
Vid ioſurs funder
Bruſtu brander
Vid blar rander.

II.
Hlam bryn ſodull
Vid bialmrodull
Beit benkreſill
Thad var blodrefill
Fra eg ad felle
Firer fetils ſuelle
Odins eike
I iarn leike

Annad ſtaf.
Tha var odda-at
I eggia gnat
Ordtyr of-gat
Eirekur at that

Thridia ſtefiamal.
I.
Raud bilmer bior
That var brafn-agior
Fleinn bitte fior
Flugu dreyrug ſpior
Ol Flagds gota
Tharbiodur ſkota
Trad nift Nara
Nattuerd ara.

II.
Flugu bialldurs tranar
Um biors lanar
Varu blode vanar

[94]

Ben-mæl-granar
Tha er oddbrekke
Sleit und-freke
Gniide hrafne
O hufudtafne

Thridie ftef.
Kom grydar ſkiae
A galfrar lae
Baud ulfur hrae
Eirikur um ſae

Fiorda ftefiamal.
I.
Beit flenn fioginn
Tha var fridur loginn
Var almur dreiginn
Thui vare ulfur feiginn
Bruſtu broddar
Bitu oddar
Baru horvar
Af bokum orvar

II.
Verpur broddſlete
Med baugſete
Hiorleik huate
Hann er blodſkate
Throaſt hier ſem huar
Hugat mæle eg thar
Freitt er auſtur um mar
Eireks op far

Fiorda ftef.
Jofur ſueigder
Hrunu unda br
Baud ulfum hrae
Eirikur um ſae

z

Fimta ftefiamal.
I.
Enn mun eg vilia
Fra verium ſkilia
Skafleik ſkata
Skal mærd huata
Laetur ſnot-ſaka
Um ſud fri vaka
Enn ſkers aka
Skyd geirs braka

II.
Brytur bog huita
Biodur hram-thuita
Muna hodd-ofa
Hring briotar lofa
Gladdiſt fiotnafiol
Vid freda miol
Miok er hilme fol
Haukſtrandar mol.

III.
Stodſt folk eige
Firer fur leige
Gall r boge
Ad eggtoge
Verpur af brondum
Enn Jofur lodum
Helldur Hornklofe
Hann er næſtur lofe

Alyktan drapunnar.
I.
Jofur eigge at
Hae eg dylia fat
Gott dottunſt that
Er eg thagu ofgat
Hraerda eg munne
Af munar grunne
Odins aege a Jorufaege

[95]

II.
Bar eg theingils lof
A thagnar rof
Kan eg maela miot
I manna fiot
Or hlatra ham
Hradur ber eg gram

Sa for that fram
Ad fleftur opnam

Nu fylger ofkan a effer
Niota bauga
Sem brage auga
Vagna vara
Edur vile tara.

IV.

THE ISLANDIC ORIGINAL

OF THE

FUNERAL SONG OF HACON.

V. Snorro Sturlefon Hift. Regum Septentrion. fol.
pag. 163.

HACONARMAL

" *Eyvindur Scalldaspillir orti quæthi eitt um fall Ha-
conar kongs, oc fua that huerfo honum var fagnat i Val-
holl; that ero kollut HACONARMAL, oc er thetta
upphaf.*"   *Snorro Sturlef. Hift.*

G Aundul ok Skogul
    Sendi Gauta Tyr
At kiofa um konga,
Huer Yngva cettar,
Skylldi meth Othni fara,
I walholl at vera.

    Brothur fundo thær Bi-
        ornar
I Brin's fara
Kong hina kozfama,
Kominn und Gunnfana,
Drupto Dolgar,

Enn Darrathur hriftiz
Upp var tha hyldur ofha-
        finn.
    Het a Haleygi,
Sems a Haimrhygi,
Jarla Einhani,
For til Orofio,
Gott hafthi hinn gaufgi
Geingi Northmanna,
Eythir eythana
Stoth und Ar-hialmi.

    Hrauthz or Herrvathom,

[96]

Hratt a vell Brynio,
Vifi verthurgar,
Athur til Vigs tæki,
Lek vith Liothmaugo,
Skylkhi land verja,
Gramur hinn glath-veri,
Stoth und Gullhialmi.

Sua beit tha Suerth,
Or Siklings Hendi,
Vathir Vafathar,
Sem i Vatni brigthi,
Brokotho Broththar,
Brotnotho Skildar,
Glumrotho Glymringar,
I Gotna Haujom.

Tranthhoz Taurgur,
Fyir Tys ok Baugo,
Hialta Harthfotom,
Haufi Northmanna,
Roma varth i Eyjo,
Rutho Kongar,
Skirar Skiald bergir,
I flatna Blothi.

Brunno Benzidar,
I bluthgom andom,
Luta Laug-berthar,
At Litha Fiovoi,
Suarathi fargymir
A fuertha nefi
Fill floth jilina,
I fiovo Storthar.

Blenthuz vith vothnar,
Vathir Ranthar Himni,
Slogdar vothur
Leko vith fkys um baugo,
Unuho Oththlar

I Othins vethri,
Hneig margt Manná;
Fyri Mækis Straumi.

Sato tha Doglingar,
Meth Suerth umtoginn,
Meth fcartha Scioltho,
Oc fcotnan Brynjor,
Vara fa Herr,
I Hugom,
Er atti til Valhallar vega:

Gaunthul that mællti,
Studdiz Geir fcapti,
Vex nu Goingi Gotho,
Er Haconi hafa,
Meth Her micinn,
Heimbauth umbothit.

Vifir that heyrthi
Huath Valkyrior,
Mælto mærar,
Af Mars Baki;
Hyggilega leto,
Oc hialmathar flotho,
Oc hofthoz Hlifar for.
[con]
Hvi thu fua (quath Ha-
Gunni Sciptir, [thom,
Geirfcaugol vorom,
Tho verthor gagns fra Go-
Ver thui vaullikom (quath
Scaugol)
Er thu velle hellz
Enn thinir fianthur flugo.

Ritha vit nu fculom,
Quath hin rika Scaugol,
Grona Heima Gotha,
Othni at figa

[97]

Her mun Allvallthur koma,
Oc hanu fialfann at fia.

    Hermothor oc Bragi,
Quath Hropta Tyr,
Gangit i gogn Grami,
Thui at Kongur fer fa,
Er Kappi thickir,
Til Hallar hiunig

    Ræfir that mællti,
Var fra Romo kominn,
Stoth allur i drora drifinn;
Illuthigurmioc,
Thykir ofs Othinn vera,
Siam ver um hant hugi.

    Einheria Grith,
Thu fcallt allra hafa,
Thigg thu at Afum Ou
Jarla Bagi
Thu att inni her
Atta Brothur, quath Bragi.

    Gerthar varar,
Quath hinn gothi kongur,
Viliom ver fialfar hafa,
Hialm oc Brynio
Scal hyriha vel,
Gott er til Geirs at taca.

Tha that kynthiz,
Hue fa kongur bafthi,
Vel of thyrmt Veom,
Er Hacon batho,
Heilann kema,
Rath oll oc Reginn.

    Gotho dogri
Verthur fa Gramur um bo-
    rinn,
Er fer getur flican fefa,
Hanns alldar,
Ae mun vera,
At gotho getit.

    Mun obunthinn,
A yta Siot,
Fenris Ulfur fara,
Athur infn gothur
A autha tranth,
Kongs Mathur komi.

    Deyr fe
Deyia frænthur
Eythiz Land oc Lath,
Sizt Hacon,
Meth Heythin Goth,
Morg er thioth um thiath.

[A different copy of part of the above poem, containing many variations, may be found in Bartholin's
Caufæ contemptæ a Danis mortis. Lib. 2. Cap. 11. p.
520.]

            H   V. THE

[98]

V.

THE ISLANDIC ORIGINAL

OF THE

COMPLAINT OF HAROLD.

V. Bartholin. de caufis contemptæ a Danis mortis.
Hafniæ 1689. pag. 154.

" *I theffum ferdum orti Haralldr gamanvifur, ok era
xvj faman, ok eitt nidrlag at ollom, tho ero herfar rit-
nar.*"
Knitlinga Saga.

Snid fyrir Sikeley vida
Sud varnm tha prudir
Brunn fkreid vel til vanar
Vengis hiortr und drengium
Vætti ek midr at motti
Muni enn thannig renna
Tho lætr gerdr i gordum
Gollhrings vid mer fkolla

Fundr var thefs at thrændir
Their hofdu lid meira
Vard fu er ver of giordum,
Vift errilig fnerra
Skildumz ungr vid ungan
All valld i ftyr fallinn
Tha let gerdr i gordum
Gollhrings vid mer fkolla.

Senn iofum ver fuanna
Sextan tha er brin vexti
Dreif a hladna hufa
Hum i fiorum rumum

Vietti ek minnr at motti
Muni enn thinnig nenna
Tho lætr gerdr i gordum
Gollhrings vid mer fkolla.

Ithrottir kann ek atta
Ygs fet ek lid at fmida
Færr er ek hvaft a hefli
Hefik fund numit ftundum
Skrida kann ek a fkidum
Skyt ek ok ræk fva at nytir
Tho lætr gerdr i gordum
Gollhrings vid mer fkolla.

Enn munat Eckia
Ung ne mær at værim
Thar er giordum fuip fuerda
Sudr i borg um morgin.
Ruddumz um med oddi
Eru merki thar verka
Tho lætr gerdr i gordum
Gollhrings vid mer fkolla.

[99]

Fæddr var ek thar alma
Upplendingar bendu.
Nu læt ek vid fker fkolla
Skeidr bummonum leidar

Vitt hefi ek fizt ytum
Eigard fkotid bardi
  Tho lætr gerdr i gordum
Gollhrings vidmerfkolla.

THE ISLANDIC ORIGINAL
of the VERSES quoted pag. 10.

—*Bith ofur capp,*
Auftur konga,
Sigars io,
Er eynar Yngva,
Menglaututh
Bith meith reitho.

Binga meithur,
Thar er vikur deilir:
Thar er Fiolkunnur,
Um fylkis hror,
Steine merktur,
Straumeyiar ues.

Oc nareithur
A nefe druther,

Snorro Sturls. Hift. p. 28.

THE ISLANDIC ORIGINAL
of the VERSES quoted pag. 80.

Tafl em ek aurr at efla,
Ithrottir kann ek niu,
Tyni ek tradla runum,
Tid er mer bok, ok fmider,

Skrida kann ek a fkidum,
Skyt ek, ok ræ fuo nytir,
Huortveggia kann ek byggiu
Harpflatt ok brag thatta.

Ol. Wor. Lit. Run. p. 129. Par.h. Cauf. &c. p. 420.

2

ADDITION to pages 9, 10.

Since the foregoing sheets were printed off we have met with a passage in
Olaus Wormius's *Monumenta Danorum,*
which seems to clear up the difficulty.
This accurate writer, observes that it
was the general practice with the ancient
Danes to bury their dead in open plains
under hillocks of earth, which they frequently also surrounded with circles of
large stones: yet acknowledges that instead of stones these *barrows* or *tumuli*
are sometimes found incircled with large
trees, disposed with great exactness; and
that these are supposed to be the sepul-
chres of kings.——"*Interim dissimulare non
possum, colles et tumulos ejusmodi etiam in
planis reperiri, grandibus undique in coro-
nam cinctos arboribus, fagis, quercubus,
aliisque lapidum vices sustinentibus, studio
et arte eleganter dispositis: in quibus regum humata esse cadavera credunt.*"

Mon. Dan. Hafn. 1643. folio. p. 38.

F I N I S.

1. Percy borrowed this book from Lord Sussex's library on 3 October 1761 and returned it on 14 August 1762, according to Bodleian MS Percy c. 9, f. 95v.

Percy's Translations
of Old Norse Poetry
in Bodleian MS Percy c. 7

1. Translations from the works of Viking Age skalds

Among Thomas Percy's draft translations in MS Bodley Percy c. 7 are four sets of verses from skaldic poetry that he found in Johan Peringskiöld's edition of Snorri Sturluson's *Heimskringla* ('Circle of the World'), a history of the kings of Norway, written c. 1230 (Whaley 1993b). Peringskiöld's edition, *Heimskringla, Eller Snorre Sturlusons Nordländske Konunga Sagar*, was published at Stockholm in 1697, and contained a parallel Icelandic text with Swedish translation, together with a Latin translation at the bottom of each chapter or page.[1] It was the first printed edition of this Old Icelandic text ever to have been published and thus was of considerable importance in the history of Old Norse-Icelandic studies, because it made available not only Snorri's many biographies of

---

[1] According to Peringskiöld's preface to the reader of his edition, an Icelander, Guðmundur Ólafsson (c. 1652-1695), was responsible for the translation from Icelandic to Swedish, but he wrote that he himself sometimes made substantial alterations to Guðmundur's text in order to give it an idiomatic character and that he produced the Latin translation himself, in response to a royal request and mindful of the potential foreign readership for the book. He admitted that he had made some stylistic changes, especially to what he terms 'sermo mythologicus', possibly a reference to skaldic diction. Both the Swedish and Latin translations show a good comprehension of the meaning of the poetry, though they do not understand everything correctly and take a reductive approach to kennings and other kinds of skaldic diction. The main manuscript upon which the edition was based is never specified, but Bjarni Aðalbjarnarson (1951, xcvii) thinks that it is likely to have been the transcript of Kringla (K) made by the Icelandic copyist Jón Eggertsson (Sth. 18 fol.). See further Clunies Ross 1998, 79-80.

the early kings of Norway, but a large amount of Old Norse poetry in addition, much of it in skaldic measures.

This invaluable resource had also been Percy's main source for *The Funeral Song of Hacon* (*Hákonarmál*) in *Five Pieces of Runic Poetry*, as has been discussed in the Introduction, and it is very likely that he translated the following pieces, most of them published here for the first time, about the time when he made the acquaintance of *Hákonarmál* in Peringskiöld's edition. As has been mentioned in the Introduction, this is very likely to have been in or before September 1760, when he sent a letter to William Shenstone enclosing 'an ancient Celtic, (or rather Runic) Poem, translated from the Icelandic', almost certainly *Hákonarmál*, together with 'some smaller Fragments of the same \kind/',[2] which are the *lausavísa* by Þjóðólfr of Hvinir (No. 1.1 below) and stanzas 6-7 of Eyvindr skáldaspillir's *Háleygjatal*, printed below as the first part of No. 1.2. The reasons for these surmises have been set out in the Introduction. I think it probable that the translation of 1.3, stanzas 7-11 of Einarr skálaglamm's *Vellekla*, was made at roughly the same time as the second pair of stanzas from *Háleygjatal* (11-12), as they follow them directly in the text of *Heimskringla*. I also presume that 1.4, a translation of stanzas 7-11 of Þorbjǫrn hornklofi's *Haraldskvæði* (or *Hrafnsmál*) was made at roughly the same time as 1.3. It occurs straight before the second set of verses of 1.2 in Percy's manuscript, on f. 32r, and 1.3 follows 1.4 on f. 33r and v.

Percy seems not to have owned Peringskiöld's edition of *Heimskringla* himself. Instead, he probably borrowed it, along with other books on Old Norse subjects, from his neighbour Edward Lye at Yardley Hastings. The evidence for this supposition is to be found in another Percy manuscript in the Bodleian Library, MS Percy c. 9, which comprises several small exercise books and papers containing records of the books Percy owned, bought and borrowed at various times of his life. Sometimes he also records the date of borrowing or purchase, the person from whom he borrowed or bought the item, and the date of return. On f. 99r there is a heading 'Revd. Mr. Lye', and underneath it, on ff. 99r and v, a list of

---

[2] These quotations are from a letter from Percy to William Shenstone, later dated by him 'September 1760' (the beginning is missing), in BL MS Add. 28221, *Correspondence between Rev. T. Percy and W. Shenstone 1757-1763*, ff. 48r-49v at 49r. The letter is No. XXIV in Brooks 1977, 70-71. The postscript to the letter, from which texts 1.1 and 1.2 (first two stanzas) are taken, was removed by Percy after Shenstone's death, and is now Bodleian MS Percy c. 7, f. 2r and v.

mainly Scandinavian books Percy borrowed from him. The entry 'Snorro Sturleson fol.' probably refers to Peringskiöld's edition of *Heimskringla*, which Lye is likely to have obtained from one of his many Swedish correspondents and colleagues.[3] The entry is crossed through, suggesting that Percy had returned the book, but it is not clear whether a date of return given higher up the list as 3 July 1761 applies to this volume too. I suspect it would not be too far from the mark to surmise that Percy had completed his translations of all the poetry he took from *Heimskringla* by mid-1761, and possibly earlier. If this proposed chronology is correct, it puts this group of translations from skaldic verse amongst the earliest Percy undertook (see the suggested chronology of Percy's translations of Old Norse poetry at the end of the Introduction).

---

[3] There is clear evidence from Edward Lye's correspondence that he asked his Swedish friends to obtain for him 'one of those Islandic Authors publish'd by Peringskiold' (Clunies Ross and Collins forthcoming, Letter 53, EL to Carl Jesper Benzelius, 5 March 1741). Unfortunately, a parcel of books intended for Lye, which included 'Snorronis Sturlesoni historia', appears to have been lost between Sweden and England, though Lye may have obtained it on a second attempt (Letter 66, Eric Benzelius to EL, 17 September 1742).

1.1 *Lausavísa* by Þjóðólfr of Hvinir[1]

PS[a] It will be difficult to meet with many Celtic pieces so well preserved & so intire as *the Epicedium of Haco*; or *the Incantation of Hervor* [in Dryden's Misc.][2] because they are only to <be> met with inserted[b] as Vouchers to Facts, in some of the Old Gothic Prose Histories. It will be more easy to meet with smaller fragments, which every where abound in those Histories. Will it be worth while to select some of the best of these, such <as> are[c] most independent & detached, in order to *fill up* our Collection?[3] – Will it be worth while to take in such as the following? ~~I think not by any Means~~[4]

(*)

Gaudrode[d5]

King of Norway being about to set sail in the

Storm in which he perished, was thus ad-

-dressed by Thiodolph his Scalde, or Poet.

[p.115][6]

Go not hence Gaudrode, through the vast ocean;

Before the Winds have given the Seas to grow calm:

Even now they strew the road[e] of Gritar[f7] with rocks

Even now the billows furiously rage & boil.

O renowned King wait here till the Seas are calmed

Abide with us till the favourable breezes blow

The Sea now rages on the Shores of Iadar[g]

a. The postscript and following translation are now f. 2r of Bodleian MS Percy c. 7. Together with the first 2 verses of 1.2, they originally formed an attachment to a letter from Percy to William Shenstone of September 1760, now BL MS Add. 28221, ff. 48r-49v, published by Brooks 1977, 69-71. The attachment was first published by Margaret M. Smith 1988, 473. Her readings, where they differ from mine, are recorded (S) in these textual notes. For all the following translations, Percy's underlinings have been rendered as italics, and I have kept his punctuation, spelling and lineation, except in the text of the postscript in 1.1, where the lineation of the ms is not observed.

b. only to <be> met with inserted] only to met with \inserted/

c. such <as> are] such are

d. Gaudrode] Gandrode S passim

e. road] ~~way~~ road

f. Gritar] Gritar S

g. Iadar] Iadar S

1. A *dróttkvætt lausavísa* from *Haralds saga hárfagra* ch. 34 in Snorri Sturluson's *Heimskringla*, there attributed to Þjóðólfr of Hvinir, a Norwegian skald active c. 900 (on him, see Clunies Ross 1993). For modern editions of the saga and the verse, see Bjarni Aðalbjarnarson I, 1941, 139, and of the verse alone Finnur Jónsson 1912-15 A I, 21 and B I, 19; Smith 1989, PeT 28, Clunies Ross 1998, 89-90, no. 8. In the notes to the translations below, I cite the texts of the verses from Bjarni Aðalbjarnarson's edition, which sometimes differs from Finnur Jónsson's. However, when Peringskiöld's Icelandic text has a reading which differs from that of Bjarni, and makes a difference to the translation, this is noted.

2. *The Epicedium of Haco* (*Hákonarmál*) was renamed *The Funeral Song of Hacon* when it appeared in *Five Pieces*. *The Incantation of Hervor*, in the translation first published in George Hickes's *Thesaurus* (1703-5) I, 193-5, was republished in *Dryden's Miscellany* 6 (1716), 387. Percy had borrowed *Dryden's Miscellany* from Lord Sussex's library, and returned it on 11 July 1761 (see chronological table in Introduction). Note that at this early date (1760) Percy is still using the word 'Celtic' to refer to Old Norse texts.

3. 'our Collection': for a discussion of what Percy might be referring to here, see Introduction, pp. 6-7.

4. This line was identified by Smith (1988, 473 and 476, n. 17) as in Shenstone's hand. It expresses his strong disapprobation of such poetry as this and other skaldic fragments, a view that he made explicit in a letter to Percy of 1 October 1760 (see Introduction, p. 8). Percy was presumably responsible for the scoring through of this line and for removing the postscript from his collected correspondence with Shenstone and placing it in his scrapbook of translated fragments from Old Icelandic.

5. 'Gaudrode': the form of the name is Gudrodus or Gaudraudus (both forms occur) in the Latin text of Peringskiöld's edition, the Old Icelandic name being Guðrøðr (Guþrauþur in Peringskiöld's Icelandic text). Guðrøðr ljómi was a son of King Haraldr hárfagri and, according to this chapter of the saga, the foster son of the poet Þjóðólfr, with whom he was spending the winter. The context of the stanza is that

Guðrøðr decides to sail north to Rogaland, even though great storms were blowing. Þjóðólfr tries to dissuade him, but in vain, and he, his crew and his ship are smashed to pieces off the coast of the notoriously treacherous Jaðarr (Jæren).

6. This reference is to Percy's source, Johan Peringskiöld's *Heimskringla, Eller Snorre Sturlusons Nordlänske Konunga Sagar*...(Stockholm, 1697), where the stanza does indeed appear on p. 115.

7. The Old Icelandic has *Geitis veg(r)* 'the road of Geitir[sea king] [SEA]'. As both the Icelandic and Latin texts in Peringskiöld read Geitir (L. *viam Geiteri*), and the Swedish translation does not translate the kenning exactly, it seems that Percy was somewhat careless in his copying.

Notes on Percy's translation

As with all his translations from Peringskiöld's edition of *Heimskringla*, Percy depends largely on the Latin translation, which is often closer to the Icelandic or more detailed than is the Swedish version. I have assumed that Percy was unable to read Swedish and so probably did not use the Swedish translation. However, his friend and neighbour Edward Lye definitely could read Swedish, as the evidence of his correspondence makes abundantly clear (Clunies Ross and Collins forthcoming), so it may have happened from time to time that the Swedish version was consulted.

Percy follows the first part of the Latin translation fairly closely, 'Ne abeas hinc Gaudraude per ingens mare, prius quam venti placata dant maria: Iam enim sternunt viam Geiteri lapidibus (i. e. maria fluctibus impetuose æstuant.)' This renders the first *helmingr* (first four lines) of the Icelandic *vísa*. Percy's version adds the explanatory 'even now the billows furiously rage and boil' as a way of conveying what the Latin has in parentheses, both obviously compensating for the reader's likely lack of understanding of the third line of the Icelandic text with its kenning, *verpr Geitis vegr grjóti*, 'Geitir's road [SEA] throws up stone'. Neither the Latin nor the Swedish translations (and therefore not Percy either) attempt to render the kenning *fleyja flatv ǫllr*, 'flat plain of the floaters' [SEA] in the first and second lines of the Icelandic.

In the second *helmingr* Percy again follows the Latin, neither fully conveying the flavour of the Icelandic compound *vindbýsna*, 'wind-signs' in line 5. In the last line, the terse *nú's brim fyr Jaðri*, 'now there's surf off Jæder', meaning that it will be worse there than in the more sheltered waters of Þjóðólfr's home (presumably in Vestfold), the Latin, followed by Percy, offers the explanatory 'Nunc ad latus provinciæ Iadar mare æstuat'.

1.2 *Háleygjatal* stanzas 6-7 and 11-12, by Eyvindr Finnsson skáldaspillir[1]

Take another small Fragment

on the Death of King

Guthlauge[a]

O![b] *Guthlaug* the subduer of the furious steed of Sigar.[2]

The Kings of the East contended together with raging wrath

When they hanged on a Tree

The munificent King, the Son of *Yngvon*[3]

And on yonder[c] Promontory stands that aged tree

From which the body of the King was suspended.

Where the Promontory *Straumyernes*[4] divides the Gulf

There I say exposed to the Winds stands that aged tree

So famous for the Tomb & Monument of the King.

And the rulers of the Earth [the sons of *Gunhilde*] spoiled[d]

Sigurd of Life.[5]

He who had given[e] to the swans of Odin [i.e. to the greedy

ravens] to drink freely

The blood of renowned warriours[f] flowing from their

wounded bodies

Had given them to drink in the farm *Oglo*

And the intrepid prince lost his life

Where the forest wood with[g] a great crackling was

consumed[h] to ashes

At what time the rulers of the Kingdome

deceived this offspring of *Thor*[6] by a broken ?Signe[i]

a. Guthlauge] Guthlange S (*passim*) As with 1.1, the first two stanzas of 1.2 were part of a postscript to a letter Percy wrote to William Shenstone in September 1760 (see footnote 1 above and note a to 1.1 for details). They now form f. 2v of Bodleian MS Percy c. 7. There is another, alternative version of the second stanza at the bottom of f. 4v of MS Percy c. 7 (quoted in note 2 below). The third and fourth stanzas are on f. 32v of the same ms. Here the number '176' appears in the top right-hand corner, and refers to the page in Peringskiöld's edition on which verses 3 and 4 begin. Percy published a slightly different version of stanzas 1 and 2 in the 'miscellaneous observations' that he prefaced to *The Incantation of Hervor* in *Five Pieces of Runic Poetry* (q.v. pp. 9-10, where the attribution to Peringskiöld's edition of *Heimskringla* is made). Stanzas 1 and 2 have also been published by Smith 1988, 473, and variations between her readings and mine are given here marked S. Stanzas 3 and 4 have not previously been published.

b. O!] \O!/ Immediately before the first line Percy began an alternate first line which he scored through: 'It was Guthlaug subdued the furious steed of Sigar'

c. yonder] yon S

d. spoiled] ~~deprived~~ spoiled

e. After 'given' Percy has inserted \~~to drink~~/

f. after 'warriours' Percy has written \[^the blood]/. I have assumed he intended to delete it.

g. wood with] wood ~~is~~ with

h. was consumed] \was/ consumed

i. by a broken ?Signe] ~~with~~ by a broken ?Signe; reading of last word uncertain

1. Four verses (6, 7, 11 and 12) in *kviðuháttr* metre from Eyvindr Finnsson skáldaspillir's *Háleygjatal*, a poem celebrating the dynasty of the Norwegian Jarls of Hlaðir, composed in honour of Jarl Hákon after his victory over the Jómsvíkingar in 985. Eyvindr was a tenth-century Norwegian skald (see Marold

1993a). Verses 6 and 7 are quoted in ch. 23 of *Ynglinga saga*, the first part of Snorri Sturluson's *Heimskringla*, and attributed to Eyvindr (ed. Bjarni Aðalbjarnarson I, 1941, 44; the numbering of stanzas follows that of Finnur Jónsson 1912-15 A I, 69 and B I, 61). Verses 11 and 12 are quoted by Snorri in ch. 6 of *Haralds saga gráfeldar*, also in *Heimskringla*, and introduced with the words 'Eyvindr skáldaspillir segir svá í Háleygjatali' (ed. Bjarni Aðalbjarnarson I, 1941, 207-8; Finnur Jónsson 1912-15 A I, 69-70, B I, 61-2). Smith 1989 includes stanzas 1 and 2 (6 and 7) under PeT 44 and 3 and 4 (11 and 12) under PeT 21, 3; they are Clunies Ross 1998, 88-9 and 91, nos. 6 and 10. As with all the other skaldic verses published in Section 1, Percy's source was Peringskiöld's 1697 edition of *Heimskringla*, where stanzas 1 and 2 are on p. 28 and 3 and 4 are on pp. 176-7.

2. Stanzas 1 and 2 (*Háleygjatal* 6 and 7) are cited by Snorri to support his prose narrative of how Guðlaugr, king of the people of Hálogaland, was hanged by Jǫrundr and Eiríkr, sons of King Yngvi Alreksson, and his body later buried in a mound (*haugr*) by his own men. It was almost certainly this last detail and possibly the information about the hanging that attracted Percy to the verses in the first place; however, the fact that he described them as a 'beautiful fragment of an ancient runic poem' (see below), indicates that he took aesthetic pleasure in them too. The alternative version on fol. 4v (which is probably a draft for what appears in *Five Pieces of Runic Poetry*, pp. 9-10) reads as follows: 'It was customary with the Northern Nations to bury the dead under a Mound of Earth \but I <?do not> know that any author mentions that they chose to do it/ at the roots of ~~some~~ trees. \In the Hist./ of Snorri Sturleson we have ~~the following~~ beautiful fragm. of an ancient runic poem, ~~which may be thus translat~~ makes mention of this practice, but seems to be of too particular to ~~be applicable to~~ prove that the practice was general – The Eastern Kings contended together with violent fury

When ~~they hanged~~ the sons of Yngvon hanged the generous
king on a tree.

And there on a promontory is that ancient tree
~~From~~ On which the dead body was suspended
Where the promontory called Straumeyernes divides the bay
There'

3. 'the Son of *Yngvon*': Percy betrays his ignorance of Icelandic grammar here. The Icelandic text has *Syner Yngva*, in which *Syner* is nom. pl. and *Yngva* is gen. sg. of *Yngvi*, properly rendered in the Latin by *Yngvonis filii*. He takes his nom. from the Latin form. The draft quoted in n. 2 above, however, shows he was undecided about it. This draft also correctly makes the sons plural and not singular, and so gets the subject of the clause right too, whereas in the translation on f. 2v (which is probably

earlier than that on 4v) 'the son of Yngvon' is construed as in apposition to 'the munificent King' and not, as it should be, to 'they'.

4. 'the Promontory *Straumyernes*': the word *nes*, 'promontory' occurs as a simplex in line 2 of this verse, but Percy introduces it again here, presumably to ensure that his potential readers understood that the place name referred to a promontory. The Icelandic text prints *Straumeyiar nes* as two words, and the Latin glosses 'ubi promontorium Straumeyernes dictum, sinus dividit', 'where the promontory called Straumeyernes divides the bay'.

5. Stanzas 3 and 4 (*Háleygjatal* 11 and 12) describe the manner of death of Sigurðr Hákonarson, Jarl of Hlaðir. He was burnt to death while taking part in a feast at Qgló in Stjóradalr (Stjørdal), betrayed to his enemies, the sons of Gunnhildr and King Eiríkr Bloodaxe, by his own brother Grjótgarðr.

6. 'this offspring of Thor': the Icelandic text and Swedish and Latin translations clearly have variants of the name of the god Týr not Þórr. The reference is to Týr as god of war, and by extension, to Jarl Sigurðr, as the Latin makes plain with the alternative 'Tyri seu Martis progeniem'. Perhaps Percy thought Týr would be unfamiliar to his readers, and so substituted Thor.

Notes on Percy's translation

Percy is not very successful in construing the grammar and syntax of stanza 1 (6), and may have been misled by the ablative absolute of the Latin's rendering of lines 3-4 of the Icelandic, *við ofrkapp austrkonunga*, 'on account of the superior force of the kings from the east', which, while not wrong, might not have helped him understand the way in which this intercalary phrase modifies the main clause *En Guðlaugr/grimman tamði/ Sigars jó* (lines 1, 2 and 5), 'But Guðlaugr tamed the grim steed of Sigarr', a way of saying the Guðlaugr was hanged. The 'steed of Sigarr' is a kenning for a gallows, and this is explained in parentheses in the Latin translation, '(seu patibulo suspensus est)'. Sigarr was a character in Norse legend who had a certain Hagbarðr hanged for having an affair with his daughter Signý. Unfortunately, Percy's apostrophe in line 1 is wide of the mark when it comes to the sense of lines 1-2 and 5 of the Icelandic, and we have already seen (note 3) that he does not get the grammar of the last 3 lines of the stanza right, even though the Latin 'quum Yngvonis filii munificum Regem de arbore quadam suspenderant' should have helped him here. All translations avoid confronting the kenning *menglǫ tuðr*, 'ring/necklace destroyer', [GENEROUS MAN] (line 7).

The first two lines of verse 2 (7) only approximate to the meaning of the first four of the Icelandic, *Ok náreiðr/ á nesi drúpir/ vingameiðr,/ þars víkr deilir*, 'And the corpse-bearing one, the swinging tree [GALLOWS], droops on the headland, where the bays are divided'. Percy here follows the Latin pretty closely, his 'that aged tree' translating *pervetusta illa arbor*.

Similarly, he follows the Latin closely in the last half of the stanza, and both only vaguely give the sense of the Icelandic *þar's, fjǫlkunnt/umfylkis hrǫr,/ steini merkt,/ Straumeyrarnes*, 'there is Straumeyrarnes [or 'Straumeyarnes' in one ms], widely known on account of the prince's corpse [or 'grave'], marked with a boulder.'

Much of the translation of stanza 3 (11) is correct, although Percy's line 3 is not very close to the Icelandic, and here he again follows the Latin. The trouble is caused by the compounded kenning *hinns svǫnum veitti/ hróka bjór/ Haddingja vals/ Farmatýs* (lines 2-5), 'the one [Sigurðr] who gave to the swans of the Týr [god] of burdens [ÓÐINN > RAVENS] the beer of the rook of the choicest of the Haddingjar [legendary brothers> WARRIORS >RAVEN >BLOOD]. The general sense is clear from both translations, the third line of Percy's following the Latin *qui Farmatyri seu Odini Cygnis, id est corvis rapacibus, gratis Haddingorum seu insignium bellatorum Sangvinem, e sauciatis corporibus promanantem*.

Once again, the kennings of verse 4 are not closely rendered in the Latin, which Percy follows, 'Et intrepidus Princeps vitam amisit, in sylvestris incendii telluris tumultu, hoc est, ubi sylvestria ligna ingenti strepitu in cineres vertebant...' There is a kenning for Sigurðr in lines 1, 3 and 4, *ófælinn ǫðlingr alnar orms*, 'the dauntless prince of the serpent of the arm [RING > GENEROUS RULER], and another rather obscure one for fire in line 2, *í ǫlun jarðar*, 'in the mackerel of the earth' [SNAKE/FIRE < *linnr* (= both 'snake' and 'fire')]. Needless to say, our translators found this last kenning beyond their reach.

1.3 *Vellekla* stanzas 7-11, by Einarr Helgason skálaglamm[1]

Accustomed to the Islands[a2], the handler of Swords, with a
mighty fleet[b] ready at his gates[c]
The joyful king[3] caused delays to sleep in the storms of
Gondla[4]
[i.e. he banished delay, was not idle, in the battles]
The Prover or Trier of his red shield red with blood[d] was
carried in ships of War
The Champion of Kings began to bring back his ship.[e]

To the warriour most expert in sea[f] affairs, the wind at that
time was not favourable
Neither the shower of arrows[g]
This Fighter stoutly & directly shook the Hail of the Bows
[sc. the arrows]
from his shields, or sails of his ships of War
The inexorable Warriour sustained the lives of wolves, he
procured them food.

Many Conflicts of the Whirlpools of the sea were
encountered
Before that diligent & watchful Champion [Haginn Jarl][i5]
Seized with his force & Power the eastern parts [of Norway]
To the benefit of the Inhabitants, to their fond desires.

I have clearly heard, that mighty revenge which the laudable
warlike

Chief took for [the death of] his father[j]

There the Keeper of the Waves conquered with his Sword

The Shower of swords & bows[k] rained on the lives

of the warlike princes of the provinces

A Champion[l] increased by the Shower of the Sword the

Multitude of free subjects to the Warriour

And the prince of Men, made the naval battle to increase

He multiplied the cold bodies of Men in the Storm of Odin[x]

[x] ie in the battle

a. These 5 stanzas are on f. 33r and v of Bodley MS Percy c. 7. They have not previously been published and were never used by Percy in any of his published works on Old Icelandic.

b. The word 'prepares' has been struck through after 'fleet'.

c. Immediately before the first line, Percy wrote, and then scored through, 'The Handler of Swords accustomed to the isles'

d. his red shield red with blood] \red/ shield red red with blood

e. before 'ship', shiel. has been written.

f. sea affairs] naval sea affairs

g. shower of arrows] shower of weapons [another word struck through] arrows

h. The inexorable Warriour] The In Warriour inexorable Warriour

i. [Haginn Jarl]] [Hg Haginn Jarl]

j. This line and all the rest of Percy's translation from *Vellekla* are on f. 33v, and the whole text has a large X drawn through it. The rest of the page contains notes relating to *The Incantation of Hervor*.

k. The Shower of swords & bows] The Sho Shower of bowes swords & bows

l. A Champion] A Warriour Champion

1. Verses 7-11 from the Icelandic skald Einarr Helgason skálaglamm's *Vellekla*, 'Gold Dearth', a *drápa* in *dróttkvætt* measure composed c. 986 in honour of Jarl Hákon Sigurðarson, and cited immediately after stanzas 11 and 12 of *Háleygjatal* (see 1.2 above) in chapter 6 of *Haralds saga gráfeldar* in Snorri Sturluson's *Heimskringla*. It seems likely that Percy translated both sets of verses around the

same time. They follow on immediately in Peringskiöld's edition and are on pp. 177-8. On Einarr, see Marold 1993b; for a modern edition of the Icelandic text, see ed. Bjarni Aðalbjarnarson I 1941, 208-211, and, for the verse only, Finnur Jónsson 1912-15 A I, 123-4 and B I, 118. Note that Peringskiöld, and therefore Percy, takes the *helmingr* of verse 10 as the first half of an 8-line stanza (=11), of which the first *helmingr* of stanza 11 forms the second part, and then takes the second helmingr of stanza 11 separately. Smith 1989 includes this translation under PeT 21, 3; it is Clunies Ross 1998, 91, no. 11.

2. 'Accustomed to the Islands': the Icelandic text printed in Peringskiöld's edition reads *eyvanþur*, 'island-accustomed' in line 2 rather than the *eiðvandr*, 'oath-careful, conscientious' of all modern editions and the extant mss. The Swedish and Latin translations unsuprisingly follow this lead, the Latin giving 'insulis assvetus', from which Percy takes his cue. The adjective qualifies the poetic compound *oddneytir*, '[weapon]point-user', for a warrior, in this case Hákon, Percy's 'the handler of Swords' following the Latin's 'mucronum tractator'.

3. 'The joyful king': these verses from *Vellekla* are cited by Snorri as witnesses to Jarl Hákon's military victories over the sons of Gunnhildr (see 1.2, stanzas 3-4 above) and to show how he avenged the death of his father Jarl Sigurðr.

4. 'Gondla': Percy's spelling of the valkyrie name Gǫndul, of which the gen. sg. occurs in the Icelandic text as *Gaundlar*, is influenced by the Latin 'in Gondlæ tempestatibus', from which he deduces a nominative form Gondla. He correctly construes the kenning 'in the storms of Gǫndul' as a battle-kenning, prompted by the Latin's explanatory 'id est in præliis'.

5. [Haginn Jarl]: viz. Jarl Hákon Sigurðarson. It is unclear why Percy does not give a form of the name closer to the Norse, for Peringskiöld's Icelandic prose text clearly reads *Hacon* and the Latin puts in parentheses at this point (hence Percy's parenthetical gloss) 'vigilans gladiator (Haquinus Iarlus)...'

Notes on Percy's translation

Vellekla is a complex poem and contains many compounded kennings, so that it presents a challenge even to a modern translator, not to speak of seventeenth- and eighteenth-century ones. The first of these stanzas from *Vellekla* was obviously difficult for the translators, aside from the fact that they had an Icelandic text with a different reading of line 2 from modern editions (see note 2 above). Percy simply follows the Latin translation for the most part, even to the point of reproducing its parenthetical explanations of kennings. He also reproduces its mistakes. The second *helmingr* is not well understood by the Latin translator, nor consequently by Percy, its general sense being that Hákon (*reynir rauðmána Heðins bóga*, 'the tester of the red moons of Heðinn's [Norse hero's] arms' [SHIELDS >WARRIOR]) raised his shield in order to damp down the warlike spirit of his enemies.

Similarly in the second verse, the first *helmingr* caused the translators a good deal of trouble and this is reflected in the poor sense of Percy's version, both on its own and in conjunction with his translation of the second *helmingr*. The Latin leads him into error again here, because the compounded kenning *sverða sverrifjarðar svanglýandr*, 'the "swan"-pleaser of the roaring fjord of swords [BLOOD>RAVEN>WARRIOR]' was too hard. However, the structure of the main clause was also misunderstood (*Vasat ... at frýja*, 'it was not [necessary] to question', sc. the king's behaviour in battle). This was turned into a statement that the king did not have a favourable wind at the time and was hampered by a shower of arrows (further misunderstandings of two battle-kennings were also involved). The second *helmingr* caused fewer problems and is probably closer to an acceptable meaning, though the warrior-kenning *hjǫrs brak-Rǫgnir*, 'noise-Rǫgnir [=Óðinn] of the sword' is turned into 'this Fighter' ('pugnator hicce'). The Latin translator, and so Percy, understood correctly a kenning for arrows (*bogna hagl*, 'hail of bows') and one for shields (*ór Hlakkar seglum*, 'from the sails of Hlǫkk[=valkyrie]'). There is some misunderstanding of the last two lines, in that the Latin translator does not realise that the second verb of the *helmingr*, *barg* (*fjǫrvi*) refers to Hákon, and means that he saved his own life. The kenning *óþyrmir varga*, 'he who does not respect wolves' also refers to Hákon. Traditionally, this has been taken as a typical warrior-kenning, of the kind 'feeder of wolves' (Finnur Jónsson B I, 118 emends to *ofþyrmir* against all mss, with the sense 'ulvenes føder'), but is more likely to refer to Hákon's harsh treatment of criminals (cf. Bjarni Aðalbjarnarson 1941 I, 210 note).

The third verse of Percy's translation corresponds to verse 9 of *Vellekla*, which is a *helmingr*. It is interesting, in terms of translation technique, that Percy produces four full lines from this half-stanza, whereas, for the three 8-line stanzas (*vísur*) that he translates, he also produces a four-line translation, though admittedly one in which the lines are usually longer. The sea-battle kenning *mart Ála él*, 'many a storm of Áli [sea king] [BATTLE AT SEA]' gives us Percy's 'Many Conflicts of the Whirlpools of the sea' by way of the Latin 'Multi gurgitum marinorum grandines, id est conflictus nautici'. The rest of the *helmingr* follows the Latin fairly closely, the latter's 'diligens atque vigilans gladiator' producing 'that diligent & watchful Champion'; the two epithets probably render the first element (*ræki-*) of the baseword of the kenning for Hákon here, *randar lauks rækilundr*, 'accomplishing tree of the leek of the shield [SWORD > WARRIOR]. There are some inaccuracies in the last two lines of the translation; in particular Percy follows the Latin in translating *at mun banda*, 'according to the gods' will', as 'To the benefit of the Inhabitants, to their fond desires' ('ad incolarum commodum ac juxta eorum desiderium').

The remaining one and a half stanzas are divided differently in Peringskiöld's edition and thus in Percy's translation from modern editions (see note 1 above). The first *helmingr* is tolerably accurately translated, though 'the Keeper of the Waves' ('maris vel fluctuum custos') misses the ship-reference in the kenning *vǫrðr hranna hrafna*. The force of the relative clause in this half-stanza is not understood, which gives Percy's second line nothing to hang onto syntactically. In the second *helmingr*, the first line gives a good general sense of the meaning without a close translation of the kennings, but the second line, 'A Champion increased by the Shower of the Sword the Multitude of free subjects to the Warriour', which follows the Latin, misses the punch-line completely, that Hákon *of jók Þundi þegns gnótt*, 'caused an abundant increase in Þundr's [=Óðinn's] thanes', that is, of warriors in Valhalla.

The final *helmingr*, which modern scholars consider the second part of stanza 11, gets the gist of the Old Icelandic, but misconstrues some parts of the syntax, especially in the last line 'He multiplied the cold bodies of Men in the Storm of Odin' ('pariter & frigida corpora quo ad vitalia, in Hari seu excelsi Odini imbre, h. e. in hoc prælio.'). The Icelandic *lét vaxa/ laufa veðr at lífum (or lífi)/ lífk ld Hóars drífu*, means 'he caused the life-cold [i.e. life-threatening] storms of Laufi [sword name] [BATTLE] to threaten the lives of the freeholding farmers with Hár's [= Óðinn's] snowdrifts [SHOWERS OF WEAPONS]'.

1.4 *Haraldskvæði* stanzas 7-11, by Þorbjǫrn hornklofi[1]

Thou hast heard how that vehement king[2] of mighty descent[a]

fought in the bay of *Hafursfiord*,[3] against *Kiotva*[4] the

wealthy:

Ships greedy of battle came from the East

With gaping heads and carved shields.[5]

They were loaded with men, [they were loaded] with white

shields.

With the arms of the western people: with Italian swords.[6]

The furious Champions[b7] roared, they had war in their hearts:

The sons of Wolves howled, the Iron resounded.

They tempted the wise, the all-powerful [king] of the

Easterlings:

Who dwelleth[c] in Utsteine:[8] Who[d] taught them to fly.

The quiet [king][9] changed the Station of his Ships, when he

had hope of the battle

There[e] was a breaking of arms, before *Haklangur*[10] fell.

The corpulent King[11] was weary of defending his kingdom.

He held the Island as a Shield, against the attacks of

Harald.[12]

The wounded men were thrown under the seats of the rowers

Their heads leaned on the keel, their backs [only] appeared[13]

The thoughtfull Men[f] were overwhelmed with stones.

> They made the Tyles of the Hall of *Suafner* to shine on their
>
> backs
>
> The inhabitants of the Eastern Mountains[14] roared;[g] from the
>
> bay of *Hafurs-fiord*
>
> They ran home thro' [the province] of Iadar, they desired to
>
> quench their thirst with mead.[15]

a. All stanzas of this translation are on f. 32r of Bodley MS Percy c. 7. They have not previously been published and were not used by Percy in any of his published works.

b. The furious Champions] The ~~Ch~~ furious Champions

c. Who dwelleth] Who ~~dwell in~~ dwelleth

d. Who] another word (illegible) has been written over 'Who'

e. There] Their

f. The thoughtfull Men] The \thoughtfull/ Men ~~deep in thought~~

g. 'murmured' has been written above 'roared', but neither is crossed through

h. they desired to quench their thirst with mead.] they desired ~~a draught~~ to quench their thirst ~~of~~ with mead.

1. The stanzas are verses 7-11, according to the conventional arrangement, of the poem *Haraldskvæði* or *Hrafnsmál*. These stanzas are quoted as a group, prefaced by the words 'Svá segir Hornklofi', in ch. 28 of Snorri Sturluson's *Haralds saga hárfagra* in *Heimskringla*, and attributed there to the late ninth-century Norwegian skald Þorbjǫrn hornklofi, 'horn cleaver' (on him, see Fidjestøl 1993). They are also in *Fagrskinna* and *Flateyjarbók*, where they are attributed to another poet, Þjóðólfr of Hvinir (see 1.1, note 1 above). The first *helmingr* of the last stanza is also quoted by Snorri in the early part of the *Gylfaginning* section of his *Edda* (Faulkes 1988, 7 and 57). The metre is *málaháttr*. Percy undoubtedly accessed the verses in Peringskiöld's 1697 edition of *Heimskringla*, where they appear on pp. 93-4 (for a modern edition see Bjarni Aðalbjarnarson 1941 I, 115-118, for a text of the verses, Finnur Jónsson 1912-15 A I, 25-6 and B I, 23). Smith 1989 includes this item as part of PeT 21, 3 and it is Clunies Ross 1998, 90, no. 9. The verses describe the victory of King Haraldr hárfagri over a combined force of his opponents in the battle of Hafrsfjǫrðr, a small fiord near Stavanger. They tell how he overcame a leader named Haklangr and then put to flight a group of men from the eastern parts

of Norway, under the leadership of a certain Kjǫtvi. The final stanzas tell in terse
and ironic fashion of how the easterners flee with their minds on their mead cups.
As Fidjestøl has commented (1993, 669), 'its vivid descriptions, grim irony, and
terse composition make it a masterpiece of skaldic poetry'.

2. 'that vehement king': Percy here follows the Latin 'Audivisti quam vehemens
ille magnæ stirpis rex pugnavit'. The Swedish has 'Huru hårt the sloges'. This
translates the Icelandic *hvé hizig barðisk*, 'how they fought there'. It is possible that
Percy identified the adverb *hizig* [*hizug* in their text] with German *hitzig*, 'quick-
tempered, violent', cf. his epithet 'vehement'.

3. 'in the bay of *Hafursfiord*': Percy here and in the last verse follows the Latin 'in
sinu Hafursfiordensi' in making the place-name explicit for non-Norse readers who
might not know what a fjord was by adding the explanatory 'bay'. The Icelandic
simply has *í Hafrsfirði*. Although the Norwegian word *fiord* appears in a small
number of late seventeenth- and earlier eighteenth-century English writings, these
are mostly in a specialist context (geography, travel writing) and the meaning of the
word may not have been widely known (cf. *OED*, *fiord*, *fjord*).

4. 'Kiotva': the form of the name comes straight from the Icelandic *við Kjǫtva enn
auðlauga*, in which Kjǫtvi is in the dative case. The Latin has 'adversus Kiotuonem
Divitem' and the Swedish 'Kiötwe', which is nearer the mark.

5. 'carved shields': the Icelandic text here has *grǫfnum tinglum*, 'with carved stem-
ornaments'. The *tingl* was an ornamented cross-piece of wood inside the stems of
Viking Age ships (cf. Wilson and Klindt-Jensen 1966, 50 and fig. 16 for an
example from the Oseberg ship). The translators obviously did not understand the
meaning of this specialised term, the Latin giving 'cælatis clypeis' and the Swedish
'utgrafna Skiöldar'.

6. 'with Italian swords': the Latin has 'Italicis ensibus' for the Icelandic *ok valskra
sverða*, where the adjective *valskr* means 'of foreign, generally southern European'
origin. The Swedish gives 'Walska' here.

7. 'The furious Champions': it is interesting that Percy refrained from using an
anglicised form of the Old Norse *berserkr* which is in the Icelandic text at this point
in the plural form *berserkir*, presumably because he did not think it would be
understood. The Latin text has it with a parenthetical explanation, 'Berserki
(furentes pugiles) rugiebant', and the Swedish has 'Slagskiämparna'. The first
citation of 'berserk' (as 'berserkars') in the Oxford English Dictionary is from Sir
Walter Scott's *The Pirate* (1822); cf. Wawn 2000, 68-70. *Ulfheðnar*, 'those
wearing wolf skins' in the following line, which also refers to the berserks, is given
in the Latin as 'luporum filii', hence Percy's 'the sons of wolves'.

8. 'in Utsteine': the form of the place-name Percy gives is once again suggested by

the Latin 'qui habitat in Utsteine', Percy not knowing enough Old Norse to realise
that the text's *at Útsteini* is in the indirect object case. The Swedish, correctly, has
'på Ut-sten', Útsteinn (modern Utstein) being the name of an island off the coast of
Rogaland.

9. 'The quiet [king]': Percy again follows the Latin 'Quietus (i. e. Rex)', this time
into error, for the Old Norse *stillir* of line 5 means 'controller, steerer', hence
'prince, king'.

10. 'Haklangur': Percy here gives the form of this name he found in the Icelandic
text, rather than the Latin 'Haklangus' or the Swedish 'Haklang'. Could he have
recognised the nominative singular of a masculine noun? Perhaps, with Lye's help.

11. 'The corpulent King': sense and word-choice follow the Latin 'corpulentem
regem', where the Swedish translation 'Then hals-tiocke Försten' is much closer to
the meaning of the Old Norse *hilmi enum halsdigra*, 'the thick-necked prince'
(dat.).

12. 'against the attacks of *Harald*': Percy does not give the nickname Lúfa for
Haraldr hárfagri, even though it was in both the Latin, 'adversante Lufo (i. e.
Haraldo rege)', and Swedish ('Harald Hårlufa') translations as well as the Old
Norse text, presumably because it meant nothing to him. This nickname was
applied to Haraldr before he won all Norway in consequence of his victory at
Hafrsfjǫrðr because he had vowed never to cut his hair until he had conquered the
whole country. The name means 'mop-head', someone with a shock of unkempt
hair.

13. 'their backs [only] appeared': slightly prudish, for *létu upp stjǫlu stúpa*, 'they
let their buttocks appear uppermost'. The Latin has 'extarent clunes'.

14. 'The inhabitants of the Eastern Mountains': here the Icelandic text has *aust
kylpar* (which is the reading of some mss) rather than the *austkylfur*, '"clubs" from
the east', eastern oafs, favoured by modern editors, hence the scornful pejorative
tone of the Old Norse is lost here on all translators.

15. 'they desired to quench their thirst with mead': Percy, following the Latin
'desiderantes mulsi haustum', does not quite convey the terse scorn of the last line
of the Old Norse *ok hugðu á mjǫðdrykkju*, 'and they thought about mead drinking'.

Notes on Percy's translation
Percy's translation of these verses from *Haraldskvæði* reads well. It has a
spirited quality which captures much of the sense of the Old Norse, and it
does not waste words. In large part he is indebted for the strict sense of the
text to the Latin translation in Peringskiöld, but he is not everywhere bound
by it. Once again, as with his other skaldic translations, two lines of

Icelandic correspond to one long line of Percy's English translation, so that he produces a four-line free verse stanza for an eight-line Norse one, in this case in *málaháttr* measure.

It is noticeable how much better the translators handle this poem in contrast to the extract from *Vellekla* in 1.3. The reason is obviously that both the syntax and the diction of *Haraldskvæði* are more straightforward and that there are only two kennings, neither of them compounded. The first, in verse 9, line 5, is not translated in the Latin, and is thus rendered by Percy by the simplex 'ships', in the clause 'changed the Station of his Ships' ('mutavit navium stationem'). However, the Old Norse reads *stǫðum Nǫkkva brá stillir*, in which there is a kenning for ships, namely *stóð Nǫkkva*, '(horse)stud of Nǫkkvi [sea-king]' [SHIPS]. The second is given its full value in the Latin, and so by Percy. It occurs in the last stanza as a kenning for the shields with which the fleeing Easterners cover their backs and involves a mythological reference to the fact that Óðinn's hall, Valhalla, was roofed with golden shields, as Snorri Sturluson explains near the beginning of *Gylfaginning*, quoting this *helmingr*. The kenning is *Sváfnis salnæfrar*, 'Sváfnir's [Óðinn's] hall-shingles' [SHIELDS], which the Latin gives as 'tegulas aulæ Suafneri (i. e. aurum sive fulgentia arma)'. It is not clear from Percy's direct translation of this phrase whether he understood the mythological reference. Although the stanza occurs in most texts of the *Gylfaginning* section of *Snorra Edda*, it was merely summarised by Mallet (1763, II, 53-4) in his French translation of Resen's 1665 edition (a copy of which was owned by Edward Lye), where the verse had been relegated to a footnote (see Clunies Ross 1998, 95-6).

2. Two translations of *Darraðarljóð*

T he fact that Thomas Percy made two draft translations of the Old Norse poem *Darraðarljóð*, 'Lay of Dǫrruðr', though he never published them, is of considerable significance in the reception history of early Norse poetry. The text of this dramatic poem had been published in 1689 and 1697 respectively by Thomas Bartholin and Thormod Torfæus (Þormóður Torfason), in each case with an Icelandic text and Latin translation, but out of the context in which it appears in medieval records, which is in manuscripts of *Njáls saga*. Bartholin quotes the poem in Chapter 1 of Book III of his *Antiquitatum Danicarum de Causis Contemptæ a Danis adhuc Gentilibus Mortis Libri Tres*, pp. 617-24, in the context of a discussion of various Old Norse beliefs in fate and doom. Torfæus cites it as part of the material he assembled from various early sources for the history of the Orkney Islands, on pp. 36-8 of his *Orcades, seu Rerum Orcadensium historiæ libri tres*.

The poem quickly achieved exemplary status among British readers as a sublime work of ancient Norse culture largely through Thomas Gray's version, and it shortly afterwards became the inspiration for visual artists such as Henry Fuseli and William Blake (Clunies Ross 1998, 118-166). Gray published his translation in 1768 as *The Fatal Sisters* in a volume of his collected works entitled *Poems by Mr. Gray*, together with his other Old Norse translation of the eddic poem *Baldrs Draumar* as *The Descent of Odin*. The evidence of his Commonplace Book in the library of Pembroke College Cambridge shows that he had completed these translations by 1761.[4] There is nothing in Percy's collection of draft translations from Old Norse in Bodley MS Percy c. 7 to indicate the date at which he composed his two translations of *Darraðarljóð*, and, as they are very different in character from Gray's, direct or even unwitting imitation of the latter's version seems most unlikely. As Percy could hardly have avoided

---

[4] For the details, and an account of how Gray came to his Old Norse studies, see Clunies Ross 1998, 105-111.

becoming aware of Gray's *The Fatal Sisters* after its publication in 1768, it seems likely that he had completed his translations some time before that date. In fact, his manuscript diary[5] seems to indicate that most of his actual work of translation of Old Norse poetry took place before 1763, that is, between September 1760, when we first find him corresponding with Shenstone on the subject, and April 1763, when *Five Pieces of Runic Poetry* was published. A further piece of evidence concerns the date on which he received his own copy of Bartholin, which was almost certainly his source, though none is given in the manuscript translation. This was on March 26, 1762 (see Introduction, *A Chronology of Percy's translations*, for the source of this evidence). Although it is possible that he had borrowed a copy of Bartholin before that time, his list of books borrowed contains no evidence of it. We may then surmise that Percy most probably made his translations of *Darraðarljóð* at some time in 1762-3 after 26 March of the former year.

Percy's two translations follow one another on ff. 34-35 of Bodley MS Percy c. 7, Version 1 being on f. 34r and v and Version 2 on f. 35r and v. Each poem is set out in columns, and the stanzas numbered. Version 1 begins at the top of the right-hand column on f. 34r, which contains stanzas 1-3, then continues on the left-hand column, then the right-hand column of f. 34v with stanzas 4-9, before returning again to 34r, left-hand column, with stanzas 10 and 11. Version 2 has only stanzas 1-3 on f. 35r (centred), and the rest, reading left-hand to right-hand column, on f. 35v. Neither poem has any heading or title, although at the head of the page (f. 34r) on which Version 1 begins, Percy has written the words 'To The Publis' and has then scored them through heavily. I assume he intended to write 'To the publisher', and then, for some reason, thought better of it. This evidence, cryptic though it is, suggests Percy may have intended Version 1 as a fair copy to be sent to his publisher, though I know of no evidence of any kind on this subject. There is no indication that he intended this poem to be included in *Five Pieces of Runic Poetry* and there is no mention of it in *Northern Antiquities*. It is certainly true that Version 1 is in a neat hand, and contains very few crossings out. It could perhaps have been intended for publication as a revision of Version 2.

In *The Norse Muse in Britain* (1998, 111-118) I made a comparison of Percy's and Gray's versions of *Darraðarljóð*, confirming what J. A. W.

---

[5] British Library MS Add. 32336, *Memoranda of Bishop Percy*. Vol. I, 1753-1778.

Bennett had asserted in his Oxford D. Phil. thesis of 1938 and in an article he published in the *Saga-Book of the Viking Society* (Bennett 1937-45, 41), that Percy's version is 'more exact than Gray's'. Bennett published the first four verses of Version 1 on pp. 259-60 of his thesis, and very recently Andrew Wawn has published the first two verses of Version 1 (2000, 29), commenting that 'Percy's response to his original is essentially prosaic, though written out in short lines. Had he decided to include it in *Five Pieces* the process of conversion to prose would have been easy.' Otherwise, apart from my own discussion in *The Norse Muse in Britain*, and the work of Bennett and Wawn noted above, no one has published or studied Percy's translations of *Darraðarljóð*. The texts and notes below are intended to support the analyses I have already made.

2.1 Darraðarljóð Version 1[1]

1[a]

Before the approaching slaughter
The cloud of arrows
Is widely scattered
The shower of blood falls
Now the ashen spear
Is knit
The web of men
Which the sisters weave
With the crimson woof
Of Randver's death.

2

The web is woven
Of human bowels
And fast to the warp
Human heads are tied
Spears bedewed with blood
Compose the treadles
The weaving instruments are steel[b]
And arrows are the shuttles
Let us close up with swords
The web of victory.

3

Forth to weave

Came Hilda & Hiorthrimul

Sangrid and Swipula

With naked swords

The spear shall be broken

The shield shall be reft in twain

And the sword

Be dashed against the buckler.

4

Weave, weave

Darradur's web.

A youthful king

First owned this sword

Let us go forth

And enter the squadrons

Where our friends

Fight with weapons[c]

5

Weave, weave

Darradur's web

And now now

Let us join the king

Gunna and Gondul

Who defend the king[d]

There have seen

Shields bedewed with blood.

6

Weave, weave

Darradur's web.

There where the arms

Of the warriors rattle

Let us not suffer him

To lose his life

The weird sisters

Preside over slaughter

7

That people

Shall rule the nations

Who heretofore inhabited

The desert promontories

Now o'er the potent king

I say death impends

The Chief[e] now falls

Beneath the arrows

8

And now a calamity

Befals the Irish

That ne'er from[f] among men

Shall be expunged

Now the web is woven

The field is bedewed with blood

The conflicts of the warriors

O'er run[g] the nations

9

Now 'tis horrible
To view around
While the bloody cloud
Flies thro' the air
The sky will be dyed
With the blood of men
Before all
Our prophecies can fail

10

Loud we sing
Of the youthful monarch
Many songs of victory
Hail to us singing
He who listens
Let him learn
And report to men
Many warlike songs

11

Let us ride on horses[h]
Bearing forth on high[i]
Naked swords
From this Place

a. Version 1 of Percy's translation of *Darraðarljóð* is on f. 34r and v of MS Percy c. 7. It may in fact, for reasons discussed above, have been the second, corrected version of the poem, and the one intended for publication. The words 'To The Publis' appear at the top left of f. 34r, above the beginning of stanza 10. F. 34 is folded lengthways down the middle to form two columns. Stanzas 1-3 are written in the right-hand column of 34r, 4-6 down the left-hand column of 34v, followed by 7-9 on its right-hand column, and the translation concludes with 10-11 in the left-hand column of 34v. The stanzas are numbered in pencil. Aside from Bennett's publication of stanzas 1-4 of Version 1 in his 1938 Oxford D. Phil. thesis (pp. 259-60), and Wawn's publication of stanzas 1-2 of Version 1 (2000, 29), neither Version has previously been published.

b. are steel] are ~~swords~~ steel

c. with weapons] with ~~swords.~~ weapons

d. the king] th king

e. The Chief] The ~~Earl~~ Chief

f. ne'er from] ne'er ~~shall~~ from

g. O'er run] O'er ~~deluge~~ run

h. there are two lines crossed through which precede this line: ~~Since we brandish/ Naked swords~~

i. Bearing forth on high] Bearing \forth on/ high

2.2 *Darraðarljóð* Version 2

1[a]

Before the approaching slaughter

The cloud of arrows

Is widely scattered.

The blood raineth

Now the spear[b]

Is applied

The ashen web of men

Which the sisters weave

With the red woof

Of Randvers death

2

The web is woven

Of human bowels

And fast to the warp[c]

Human heads are tied[d]

Spears bedewed with blood

Compose the treadles

The weaving instruments are swords[e]

And the shuttles are arrows[f]

Let us weave with swords

The web of victory.

3

Forth to weave

Come Hilda and Hiorthrimula

Sangrida & Suipula

With drawn swords

The spear shall be broken

The shield be cloven

And the sword

be dashed against the buckler

4

Weave, weave

Darradur's web.

This sword a youthful king

First possest.

Let us go forth

And enter the squadrons

Where our friends

Fight with arms.

5

Weave, weave

Darradur's web

Blind[g] to the king then

then let us cleave[h]

There Gunna & Gondula

Who defended the king

Saw the shields

Bedewed with blood

6

Weave, weave,
Darradurs web
There where the arms
Of the warriours rattle
Let us not suffer him[i]
To lose his life
The weird sisters
Preside o'er slaughter

7

That people
Shall rule the lands
Who heretofore inhabited
The Desert promontories
Now I say[j]
Death o'er hands[k]
The powerful king
The East now falls
Beneath the arrows

8

And o'er the Irish
Befals a calamity[l]
That ne'er shall be wiped
Out from men[m]

Now the web is woven

The field is bedewed with blood

The encounters of the soldiers

Will o'er run the lands

9

Now its horrible[n]

To look about

While the bloody cloud

Flies thro' the air

The sky shall \<be\> stained[o]

With the blood of men

Before our prophecies

Can fail.

10

Loud we sing[p]

Of the youthful Monarch

Many songs of victory

Hail to our songs[q]

He who listens[r]

Let him learn

And report to men

Many warlike songs

11

Let us ride on horses[s]

From this place

Since we bear

Naked swords.

a. Version 2 begins (again the sheet of paper is folded down the middle to form two columns) on the right-hand side of 35r with stanzas 1-3, the left-hand column being blank, then continues on 35v, left-hand column, with stanzas 4-7, and right-hand column (stanzas 8-11). The stanzas are again numbered in pencil. Percy has written the following lengthways along the right-hand edge of the first column of 35v, 'to be Bug – to be elate'.

b. Now the spear] Now the ~~ashen~~ spear

c. And fast to the warp] And \fast/ to the warp

d. Human heads are tied] Human heads are ~~fastened~~ tied

e. Immediately preceding this line are the following two lines crossed through: ~~The weaving instruments are of steel/ An Swords are the weav~~

f. And the shuttles are arrows] And ~~for~~ the shuttles are arrows

g. The first letter of this word seems to have been overwritten with the letter D. Did Percy intend 'bind' rather than 'blind'?

h. then let us cleave] ~~Then~~ then let us cleave

i. Let us not suffer him] Let us not ~~permit~~ him ['suffer' has been written above ~~permit~~]

j. Now I say] Now I say ~~Death~~

k. Death o'er hands] ~~O'er hangs~~ Death o'er hands

l. Befals a calamity] Befals a ~~pain~~ calamity

m. That ne'er shall be wiped/ out from men] That ne'er shall be wiped ~~out/ From men~~ out from men

n. Preceding this line are the following: '~~Now its it terrib horrible~~'

o. The sky shall <be> stained] The sky shall stained

p. The word 'About' has been written above this line and crossed through.

q. Hail to our songs] Hail to our ~~sing~~ songs

r. He who listens] He who ~~hears~~ listens

s. Let us ride on horses] Let us ride on ~~ride~~ horses

1. *Darraðarljóð* is an anonymous poem of 11 stanzas in the measure *fornyrðislag* which has been preserved in manuscripts of the Old Icelandic *Njáls saga*, the oldest being Reykjabók, MS AM 468, 4to. from c. 1300. The poem is quoted in ch. 157 of

the saga, among accounts of of several strange visions and portents that preceded the Battle of Clontarf between Brian Bóruma, High-King of Ireland, and Sigurðr, Earl of Orkney. The battle took place on Good Friday 1014.

The age and provenance of the poem itself are uncertain, though Poole (1991, 116-156 and 1993) has suggested an association with the British Isles, possibly the Orkneys, and seen similarities between its narrative technique and that of other 'running commentary' and work song-like poems such as *Liðsmannaflokkr*, which is likely to have been composed in England for King Knútr not long after his conquest of the country in 1017. *Njáls saga*, on the other hand, is usually dated somewhere between 1275-1290.

The poem is designed to praise a certain young king (cf. stanza 4/3), who has won a victory over the Irish. Whether that 'young king' was in fact the Viking leader Sigtryggr Óláfsson, King of Dublin, and an ally of Earl Sigurðr, and the battle in question the Battle of Clontarf, as the saga claims, is an open question. In the poem valkyries actively assist the young king by 'weaving' the battle, that is, by sending showers of weapons against his opponents. (For the metaphorical nature of the equivalence between weaving at a loom and fighting, see the textual commentary below). The idea of valkyries or other supernatural female figures actively assisting warriors on the field of battle occurs in other contexts in Old Norse. One of the best known is the assistance given to Jarl Hákon Sigurðarson at the famous sea battle of Hjǫrungavágr by his supernatural protectress Þorgerðr Hǫrðabrúðr, as told in *Jómsvíkinga saga* (c. 1200).

The writer of *Njáls saga* has interpreted the poem in what may be an over-literal fashion, by depicting the valkyries as actually engaged in weaving, using human body-parts instead of thread and loom-weights, in order to determine the outcome of the battle by magical means. According to the saga prose that precedes the quotation of the poem, a certain man named Dǫrruðr (for whom there is no poetic authority) went outside at Caithness and saw twelve riders approach a women's apartment (*dyngja*) and disappear inside. He walked over to a window and peered in. He saw women there with a loom set up for weaving, but, instead of weights, they were using men's heads, and instead of the thread for the weft and warp, they were using men's intestines. They had a sword for a beater and an arrow for the shuttle. He heard them chanting verses, and the poem is then presented as their song. After its quotation, the saga writer tells that the women tore the woven cloth from the loom and ripped it to pieces, each keeping the piece she held in her hands. Dǫrruðr went home and the women mounted their horses and rode away, six to the north and six to the south.

The paragraph that preceded the quotation of the poem as well as the text of the poem itself was available to eighteenth-century translators in Thomas Bartholin's *Antiquitatum Danicarum de Causis Contemptæ a Danis adhuc Gentilibus Mortis Libri Tres*, pp. 617-24, where both are quoted in Icelandic and Latin. The edited Icelandic and Latin texts are the work of Árni Magnússon, who collaborated with Bartholin on this project (Bekker-Nielsen and Widding 1972, 14-15). Þormóður Torfason used Bartholin's texts in his *Orcades*, but, after quoting the poem, he included on p. 38 a Latin translation of the saga paragraph that describes what happens after the song has been sung. The prose explication in the saga text made the poem powerfully accessible to a 'sublime' reading of its grotesque and horrifying imagery, and this certainly inspired both Gray and Percy as well as artists who read their work, like Fuseli and Blake (Clunies Ross 1998, 118-166).

For a modern edition of the poem in *Njáls saga*, see Einar Ól. Sveinsson 1954, 454-8, and, for the standard edition of the poem alone, Finnur Jónsson 1912-15 A I, 419-21 and B I, 389-91. Both versions of *Darraðarljóð* are included by Smith 1989 under PeT 21, 3; see also Clunies Ross 1998, 91, no. 12.

Notes on Percy's translation

These notes address both of Percy's Versions of *Darraðarljóð* together, because the differences between them are mainly stylistic. As I have suggested above, Version 1 is probably a 'cleaned-up' text, perhaps intended for publication.

In *The Norse Muse in Britain* (1998, 113-4) I observed that *Darraðarljóð* is a difficult poem to translate even today. The main reason for this is the pervasive metaphorical equation in the poem between the valkyries' participation in the battle and the weaving of a web of cloth. This allows it to use a series of multivalent images, sometimes expressed through kennings, which of their nature do not need to be reduced to a stark statement of their referential value. A translator, however, does not have that luxury. He must either gloss over the multivalency of the images (something most translators of Old Norse in Percy's day usually did anyway) or choose one particular set of referents over another.

Both the author of *Njáls saga* and most early modern translators and commentators, following the saga prose, understood the poem to depict the valkyries as literally weaving a magic web out of the guts of fallen warriors, using their heads as loom-weights, in order to influence the course of the battle in the 'young king's' favour. Hence their translations are fully determined referentially in this direction, whereas a reading of the poem itself reveals many places where it is not clear whether the poet is speaking literally or metaphorically. Because Percy keeps closely to the Latin translation, his version is not so heavily determined in the direction of the grotesqueries that made Gray's such an instant success with the British reading public.

Another reason why *Darraðarljóð* is difficult to translate is because it is necessary to know the various parts of the upright or perpendicular loom that was still in use in Iceland until the second half of the eighteenth century, and to realise how the various parts worked, in order to understand both the technical terms used by the poet and the weaving images he creates. Hoffmann 1964 is an exhaustive study of the warp-weighted loom and Poole 1985 has studied the weaving imagery in *Darraðarljóð*. The necessary information was clearly stated by Nora Kershaw (1922, 119-120) and is also to be found in the notes to Einar Ól. Sveinsson's edition (1954, 454-8; see especially the diagram of the loom (*vefstaður*) and its parts between pp. 458-9). Kershaw wrote:

'The root principle of all weaving is the rapid passing to and fro of a single free thread of yarn (i.e. weft thread) alternately under and over a series of parallel threads of yarn (i.e. warp threads). This process is represented by the expression *vinda vef*. To ensure a durable fabric, care must be taken in simple weaving, as in the ordinary darning stitch, that the weft thread is never placed under the same thread of warp in two consecutive passages. To facilitate the weaver's task the threads of the warp are invariably stretched and held taut, generally by weights.

In the old Icelandic upright loom the warp threads (*vefr*) are attached to a thick rounded bar of wood (*rifr*) which revolves freely in two wooden sockets at the top of two upright wooden posts (*hleinar*). A beam (*skaft*) or, later, two or even several beams, rested on wooden pegs (*skaftillir*) in the middle of the *hleinar*. To this shaft are attached the ends of a number of threads. At the unattached ends are loops through each of which is threaded every alternate warp thread. The backward and forward movement of the shaft thus serves to decussate the warp threads in much the same way as the heilds of a modern horizontal hand loom. ... The ends of the warp opposite to the *rifr* are weighted (*kljáðr*), singly or in groups, by heavy stones (*kljásteinar*), which hang freely and hold the warp taut. The work of the reed in the modern hand loom seems to have been done by different implements ... part of this work was done by the *skeið*, a large smooth spear-shaped implement of whalebone.'

Given these difficulties, and the fact that he mostly worked from the

Latin translation of the Old Icelandic poem, Percy produced a spirited, readable translation, largely free from the deliberate poetic echoes and archaisms that characterise Gray's, and one which was as close to the Icelandic as his small knowledge of the language would allow. We can assume that, for specific words and phrases, he was able to consult Edward Lye.

I have already discussed Percy's translation of the first stanza of *Darraðarljóð* in *The Norse Muse in Britain*, pp. 113-116, and will only summarise those remarks here. The first two stanzas of the poem, in particular, articulate a metaphorical equation between the activity of weaving on a loom and the conduct of a battle, which valkyries are directing. This metaphor is expressed mainly through kennings, which the Latin translation, and therefore Percy, reduce to non-metaphorical statements except for the image of 'clouds of arrows' (*sagittarum nubes*). He follows the Latin closely, his hesitation over which noun to apply the adjective 'ashen' to being caused by the obscurity of the Latin (Clunies Ross 1998, 115, n. 18). In the second half of the stanza he recognises that there is a reference to valkyries, but does not construe the kenning for them correctly, yet neither does the Latin, which has *amicæ* where he has 'the sisters'. As I have discussed elsewhere (Clunies Ross 1998, 116-117), the use of the word 'sisters' to refer to valkyries and the strong association between them and fate owes a great deal to Shakespeare's 'weird sisters' from *Macbeth*, as indeed does Gray's version, *The Fatal Sisters*, in even greater measure.

It is in the second stanza that the equation between the warp (*vefr*) woven by the valkyries from men's guts (*ýta þǫrmum*) is clearly stated. As already mentioned, the author of *Njáls saga* seems to have taken this literally to mean that a group of valkyries are sitting weaving with human entrails and using men's heads for loom weights. This is certainly the view that Gray's translation promoted but it is much less obvious in Percy's. However, it is also possible to read this stanza as a metaphorical way of saying that the valkyries are participating in the battle, sending javelins and arrows into the fray, as the last two lines make clear, *skulum slá sverðum/ sigrvef þenna*, 'we must sley this victory-web [BATTLE] with swords', or, as Percy has it, 'Let us close up with swords/ The web of victory'. His text follows the Latin closely, and his diction is plain (note the use of 'bowels' compared with Gray's 'griesly texture ... of human entrails made'), except for 'spears bedewed with blood', but this image follows the Latin 'sunt sanguine roratæ hastæ'.

The third stanza introduces several valkyries by name and continues the weaving image to describe their destructive action in battle. For some reason Percy has the correct present tense in Version 2 but has changed it to the preterite 'came' in Version 1. There is a single kenning in this verse, *hjálmgagarr*, 'helmet-dog' [SWORD], but the Latin, and so Percy, render this by a simplex. The first two lines of stanza 4 introduce a formula, *vindum, vindum vef darraðar*, 'we are weaving, weaving the web of the spear [or 'pennant']', that contains the uncommon word *darraðr*, about whose meaning there has been a good deal of scholarly debate since Percy's time (cf. Holtsmark 1939; Poole 1985). Exactly the same two lines are repeated at the beginning of stanzas 5 and 6. In translating this formula as 'weave, weave Daradur's web', Percy was following the Latin, which also makes Darradus a personal name, doubtless following the lead of *Njáls saga*. He must not have realised that the same phrase also occurs in the *Hǫfuðlausn* of Egill Skallagrímsson (5/2), and that he had translated it there as 'the web of spears' (*Five Pieces of Runic Poetry*, p. 50), following a note from his friend Lye that appears on the next page (f. 36r) of Bodley Percy c. 7, to the effect that 'darraþur exponitur Gladius'.

Stanza 5 contains no difficult language. Percy follows the Latin here, but makes a mistake when translating 'who defend the king' as present tense. It is preterite, as the Latin correctly has it, implying that Gunnr and Gǫndul have long played a special protective role on behalf of the young king. 'Shields bedewed with blood' again follows the Latin 'sangvine rorata scutæ'. In stanza 6, the rather curious 'there where the arms of the warriors rattle' translates the Latin 'ubi arma concrepant bellacium virorum', for the Icelandic *vé vaða vígra manna*, 'the battle-standards of the brave men flutter'. Percy's translation of the last two lines of this stanza as 'The weird sisters/ Preside over slaughter' is interesting, because it deliberately avoids using an anglicised version of the Icelandic *valkyriur*, which was available to him in the Latin as 'Valkyriæ'. He must have thought that the Shakespearean echo would give his readers a better idea of the role of these supernatural women, who he probably considered to be versions of the Fates of classical antiquity, than if he had given a form of the Icelandic word.[6] Thomas Gray found it necessary to provide a note

---

[6] Wawn (2000, 27-8) has drawn attention to William Collins' interest in similar themes, including that of 'Wayward Sisters' in his *An Ode on the Popular Superstitions of the Highlands of Scotland, considered as the Subject of Poetry*

explaining who valkyries were in the 1768 edition of his poems (the text is reproduced in Clunies Ross 1998, 117), and his usage is the earliest recorded by the *Oxford English Dictionary*.

With stanza 7 the narrating voice (presumably that of one of the valkyries) turns to predicting the outcome of the battle, which will bring victory to 'those people who previously occupied the outlying headlands' (*þeir lýðir...er útskaga áðr of byggðu*), presumably the Norsemen, while a powerful prince (*ríkr gramr*), possibly Brian Boruma, High-King of Ireland, has death ordained for him, 'I say death has been ordained for the mighty prince' (*kveð ek ríkum gram/ ráðinn dauða*), and an earl has been laid low by spears (*nú er fyrir oddum/jarlmaðr hniginn*). The last reference has conventionally been interpreted to refer to Jarl Sigurðr. The stanza is straightforward as far as diction and syntax is concerned, and there are no kennings. Percy follows the Latin with his 'desert promontories' (*qvi deserta promontoria antea incolebant*). His hesitation in Version 2 in translating *dico potenti regi mortem imminere* is made good by Version 1's 'Now o'er the potent king/ I say death impends'.

Stanza 8 deals with the fate of the Irish and the impact of the battle in the wider world. Percy shows some indecision in translating *angr*, 'sorrow, misfortune' (Latin *dolor*) in line 2, obviously deciding that 'pain', which was his first thought in Version 2, was too weak. In lines 4-5 of the Icelandic the speaker pronounces *Nú er vefr ofinn/ en vǫllr roðinn*, 'now the web is woven and the [battle-]field reddened'. The half-kenning *læspiǫll gota*, 'news of guileful deceit of the men' in the last line is translated as *conflictus militum* in the Latin and 'the conflicts of the warriors' by Percy.

The opening lines of stanza 9 invite poetic elaboration with their direct invocation of horror and bloody clouds gathering in the sky. Percy, keeping closely to the Latin, does not embroider. The version of this stanza that Bartholin and Árni Magnússon used had, for the last two lines of the stanza, 'adr spar varar/ springa allar', which the Latin translates as *antequam vaticinia nostra omnia corruant* which gives Percy's 'Before all/ Our prophecies can fail'. There is a difficulty of sense here, however, and modern editors have either suggested a different meaning for *springa*, as 'before all our prophecies ?are fulfilled', or adopted the readings of other manuscripts.

---

which was composed even earlier than Gray's and Percy's Norse poems (at the end of 1749), but not published until 1788.

Stanzas 10 and 11 express the valkyries' sense of triumph in the victory they have brought about for the young king. Now the emphasis is upon their vocal triumphs (*vel qvedu ver*, 'we sing well', some mss and most modern editors read *qváðu*, 'we have sung' here), and, after a line of self-congratulation (*syngjum heilar*!, 'hail to us singing!'), they urge anyone listening to them to learn their song and report it to men. The half-stanza 11 has the valkyries on the move, brandishing their swords and galloping off from the battlefield on their barebacked horses.

Percy's translation of the two concluding stanzas makes a strong but restrained statement. Clearly, he experimented between the two versions with the best way to translate the last stanza, in the end going for the order of the Icelandic text and Latin translation, which refers to the valkyries riding their horses bareback first and then to their drawn swords. Version 1's 'on high' is the only addition to the translation which is not strictly justified.

3. Extracts from the Old English *Battle of Brunanburh*

O ur chief source of information on Percy's motivation for translating
this, the sole example of Old English poetry in his collection of
otherwise exclusively Norse verse, is his correspondence with the
Welsh scholar and translator Evan Evans. The letters between the two men
have been edited by Aneirin Lewis (1957) and I have discussed elsewhere
the light they throw on both men's approach to the task of translating early
medieval poetry (Clunies Ross 1998, 56-7, 92-3). In his letter to Evans of
14 August 1762, Percy indicated that his interest in *Brunanburh* stems from
what he perceived to be its similarity to Old Norse 'runic odes':

> 'The subject [of *Brunanburh*] is a Victory gained by the
> Anglo-Saxon Athelstan over the Dane Anlafe, and his
> confederate Constantinus K. of Scotland. If you compare it
> with the Runic Ode of Regner Lodbrog, you will see a
> remarkable affinity between them: some of the phrases &
> imagery being common to both; as *the play of arms*:
> &c, &c –' (Lewis 1957, 31-2)

It also appears from the evidence of his letters to Evans that Percy had
used as the basis of his translation an Old English text and a literal Latin
version of the poem, the latter made by his friend and neighbour Edward
Lye. Two editions of *The Battle of Brunanburh* already existed, the first
being the prose version of Edmund Gibson, in his edition of the *Anglo-
Saxon Chronicle* published in 1692, pp. 112-114, and the second the
version of George Hickes, based on Gibson's edition, which was set out in
verse half-lines in the *Thesaurus* of 1703-5, I, pp. 181-2. When Percy first
mentions the poem to Evans in a letter of 15 October 1761, he indicates
that he got from Lye both the Old English text of the 'Saxon Ode' and a
literal Latin translation, and from the latter constructed his 'free' English
version (Lewis 1957, 12-13). The Latin translation from which Percy
worked was evidently Lye's own, but it is not clear which of the two
exisiting editions of the Old English Lye was using. He knew and quite
possibly used both. Percy says that he transcribed both the translation and
the original from Lye's 'curious Collections'. Somehow, this 1761 version

of the poem and Latin translation got lost, but Lye had found them again in 'the immense ocean of his papers' by July of 1762, and on August 14 Percy sent a copy to Evans, telling him that 'The Latin version falls from the pen of my very learned friend Mr Lye, who has made many important emendations in the original. The English was a slight attempt of my own to see if one could not throw a little spirit into a literal, interlinear version...' (Lewis 1957, 31-2).

It is difficult to tell how the two fragmentary versions of the poem in Percy's notebook fit in with the information he gives Evan Evans and the transcripts he apparently sent him. As one version is in prose and the other verse, it is tempting to think that they follow Gibson's prose and Hickes's verse lay-out of the Old English respectively, but this is merely guesswork. The presumably full translation of the poem that Percy sent Evans appears not to have survived, even though Evans claimed to have returned it (Clunies Ross 1998, 93). At one time Percy intended to use *Brunanburh* as an example of Anglo-Saxon poetry in an anthology of early verse that he was planning from a variety of languages, but this idea was never realised (Clunies Ross 1998, 92-3). By 1764 he had changed his plan and wrote to Evans that he would 'throw to the end of Mallet's book [*Northern Antiquities*] ...what Saxon Poems I have fit for Publication' (Lewis 1957, 98), but he never did this either. The sole use he made of his knowledge of *Brunanburh* in his published work was a footnote reference in *Northern Antiquities* (1770, II, 196)[7] to the comparability between Anglo-Saxon poetry and Old Norse skaldic versification, diction and poetic allusion.

Percy's notebook translation is on small scraps of paper, two of which (7v and 9v) also contain notes for his translation of *The Incantation of Hervor*.[8] It looks as though he made two separate attempts to translate the poem, the first in his accustomed short lines of free verse and the second in prose paragraphs. The first version is on ff. 9v (lines 1-7 of the Old English poem), 8v (lines 12b-20a) and 7v (lines 25-28b and 37-40 in two columns).

---

[7] Here Percy refers to Gibson's edition of the Anglo-Saxon text, but he must have known Hickes's also. He had borrowed Hickes's *Thesaurus* (from which he also knew *The Incantation of Hervor*) from Lye some time in 1761-2 and returned it to him (Bodleian MS Percy c. 9, f. 99r-v).

[8] This may suggest he worked on the two poems, both of which were in Hickes's *Thesaurus* (see note 7 above), at the same time, though he eventually used Verelius's edition (supplemented by Bartholin) for the Icelandic text of *The Incantation of Hervor*.

The second version is on f. 10v, and comprises lines 1-14 of the Old English poem in three prose paragraphs. The two versions are printed separately here.

3.1 *The Battle of Brunanburh* Version 1[1]

King Athelstan[a]
Lord of valiant chiefs.[b]
He that giveth gold-chains to his nobles
Together with his brother[c]
Edmund Etheling
A Prince descended of an ancient race
Smote[d] in war
With the edges of the sword
Near to Brunanburgh.
The sons of Edward
Cleaved down shields

***

The field resounded,[e]
Warriors sweated
What time the sun rising
That glorious planet
Glided over the earth
The bright taper of God
Of[f] the eternal Lord.
Till that noble creature
Revisited his Lodging[g]
There lay many Warriors
Grinded to death with darts
The Northern men
With shield shot thorough[h]
As also Scots

War's cursed Seed

***

Then was safety to none[i]

Who with *Anlafé*

Across the sea[j]

In the ship's bosom[k]

Sought the Land

Destined for the fight

Five lay

In the field of battle[l]

***

To save[m] their Lives

And there the wise old man

Constantinus

By flight returned

To his Northern country

The warlike Chief

Had need to wail

The Commerce of swords

It was the remains of his family

His friend laid prostrate

---

a. The first lines of the translation, corresponding to lines 1-7 of the Old English poem, run down to the first set of asterisks; they are on f. 9v of MS Percy c. 7.

b. Lord of valiant chiefs] Lord of ~~the~~ valiant chiefs.

c. The words '~~And also his~~' are written before the line.

d. The word '~~Struck~~' has been written before 'Smote' and another word (illegible) is crossed out above 'Smote'.

e. From here until the next asterisk, corresponding to lines 12b-20a of the Old English poem, are on Percy c. 7, fol. 8v.

f. The word 'Of' is blotted, but is legible.

g. his Lodging] his ~~abode~~ Lodging

h. shot thorough] shot ~~thro'~~ thorough

i. Then was safety to none] Thereafter ~~no~~ was safety to none. The word 'Then' has been written above 'Thereafter'. The lines between here and the next set of asterisks are in the left- hand column of f. 7v (corresponding to lines 25-28b of the Old English), and the final set of lines (37-40 of the Old English) are in the right-hand column of the same folio.

j. Across the sea] ~~Thro' the~~ Across the sea

k. In the ship's bosom] In the ship's ~~womb~~ bosom

l. The last two lines are partly erased.

m. The 'v' of 'save' has been altered from 'f'

1. The Old English poem of 73 lines, now entitled *The Battle of Brunanburh*, is found in the *Anglo-Saxon Chronicle* in 4 extant manuscripts under the annal entry for the year 937 (Campbell 1938). Percy's translation was first identified by Bennett 1938, 259-60 and 1937-45, 41. Smith (1989) includes the work under PeT 21, 2, but does not identify it precisely. It is Clunies Ross 1998, 91-3, no. 13. Percy's translations have not previously been published.

3.2 The Battle of Brunanburh Version 2

King Athelstan, Lord of the Warriours, he that giveth[a]

Chains to his nobles, and prince Edmund his brother

a prince descended from an ancient race: struck

in war with the Edges of the sword near Brunan:

burgh.

The sons of Edward, cleaved shields,[b] felled the

lofty banners, domestic reliques. Such courage did

they inherit from their ancestors, that they defended

the land, the treasures & their homes, against

all deadly foes.[c]

Hateful[d] fell the Scottish people:

and the ship-men rushed[e] to their death. The

Field of war resounded. The warriors sweat; what time

the Sun, at morning tide,[f] that glorious planet ...

a. These three prose paragraphs are all on f. 10v and give a version of lines 1-14 of
the Old English poem. I have kept the lineation of the original.
b. The words 'He cleaved shields' precede the first words of this paragraph.
c. all deadly foes.] all their all deadly foes.
d. Hateful fell] The Hateful Hat Hateful fell
e. rushed] ran to rushed
f. 'tide' possibly changed from 'time'

References

Manuscript sources

Oxford, Bodleian Library MS Percy c. 7, *Runic Poetry &c.*

Oxford, Bodleian Library MS Percy c. 9, *Notebooks of Bishop Percy*

Oxford, Bodleian Library MS Eng. Lett. d. 59, *Correspondence of Bishop Percy*

Oxford, Bodleian Library MS D. Phil. d. 287, Bennett, J. A. W. 1938, *The History of Old English and Old Norse Studies in England from the time of Francis Junius till the End of the Eighteenth Century*. Unpublished D. Phil. thesis.

London, British Library Additional MS 28221, *Correspondence between Rev. T. Percy and W. Shenstone 1757-1763*

London, British Library Additional MS 32325, *Correspondence of Edward Lye*

London, British Library Additional MS 32330, *Correspondence of Thomas Percy and Evan Evans*

London, British Library Additional MS 32336, *Memoranda of Bishop Percy, Vol. 1, 1753-1778*

Printed sources

Andersson, Theodore M. and Kari Ellen Gade trans. 2000, *Morkinskinna. The Earliest Icelandic Chronicle of the Norwegian Kings (1030-1157).* Islandica LI. Cornell University Press, Ithaca and London.

Aðalbjarnarson, Bjarni ed. 1941and 1951, *Snorri Sturluson, Heimskringla* I and III. Íslenzk fornrit vols. XXVI and XXVII. Hið íslenzka fornritafélag, Reykjavík.

Bartholin, Thomas 1689, *Antiquitatum Danicarum de Causis Contemptæ a Danis adhuc Gentilibus Mortis. Libri Tres ex vetustis codicibus & monumentis hactenus ineditis congesti.* Joh. Phil. Bockenhoffer, Copenhagen.

Bekker-Nielsen, Hans and Ole Widding, trans. R. Mattila 1972, *Arne Magnusson. The Manuscript Collector.* Odense University Press, Odense.

Bennett, J. A. W. 1938 (see under Manuscript sources)

Blair, Hugh 1763, *A Critical Dissertation on the Poems of Ossian, The Son of Fingal.* Printed for T. Becket and P. A. De Houdt, London.

Braund, S. H. trans. 1992, *Lucan Civil War.* Clarendon Press, Oxford.

Brooks, Cleanth ed. 1977, *The Correspondence of Thomas Percy and William Shenstone.* The Percy Letters VII. Yale University Press, New Haven and London.

Campbell, Alastair ed. 1938, *The Battle of Brunanburh.* William Heinemann, London.

Clunies Ross, Margaret 1993, 'Þjóðólfr of Hvin', in Phillip Pulsiano and Kirsten Wolf eds., *Medieval Scandinavia. An Encyclopedia.* Garland Publishing, New York and London, pp. 665-6.

Clunies Ross, Margaret 1994, 'Percy and Mallet. The Genesis of *Northern Antiquities*', in Gísli Sigurðsson *et al.* eds., *Sagnaþing helgað Jónasi Kristjánssyni sjötugum 10. april 1994.* 2 vols. Hið íslenzka bókmenntafélag, Reykjavík I, pp. 107-117.

Clunies Ross, Margaret 1998, *The Norse Muse in Britain, 1750-1820. With an appendix on the periodical literature by Amanda J. Collins.* Hesperides, Letterature e culture occidentali. Edizioni Parnaso, Trieste.

Clunies Ross, Margaret 1999 [1997], 'Revaluing the Work of Edward Lye, an Eighteenth-Century Septentrional Scholar', *Studies in Medievalism* IX, 66-79.

Clunies Ross, Margaret and Lars Lönnroth 1999, 'The Norse Muse: Report from an International Research Project', *alvíssmál* 9 (1999), 3-28.

Clunies Ross, Margaret, Kari Gade, Edith Marold, Guðrún Nordal and Diana Whaley 2000, *Norse-Icelandic Skaldic Poetry of the Scandinavian Middle Ages: Editors' Manual.* Centre for Medieval Studies, University of Sydney.

Clunies Ross, Margaret and Amanda Collins eds. forthcoming, *The Correspondence of Edward Lye.*

Dickins, Bruce 1962, 'Two Little-Known Renderings of the Old Norse "Waking of Angantyr"', *Saga-Book of the Viking Society* xvi, 80-88.

Faulkes, Anthony ed. 1977, *Edda Islandorum, Völuspá. Hávamál. P. H. Resen's editions of 1665.* Two Versions of Snorra Edda from the 17th. Century, Vol. II. Stofnun Árna Magnússonar, Reykjavík.

Faulkes, Anthony ed. 1988, *Snorri Sturluson Edda. Prologue and Gylfaginning.* Viking Society for Northern Research, University College London. First published by Oxford University Press, 1982.

Faulkes, Anthony ed. 1998, *Snorri Sturluson Edda. Skáldskaparmál.* 2 vols. 1: Introduction, Text and Notes. 2: Glossary and Index of Names. Viking Society for Northern Research, University College London.

Faulkes, Anthony ed. 1999, *Snorri Sturluson Edda. Háttatal.* London, Viking Society for Northern Research, University College London.

Fell, Christine E. 1996, 'The first publication of Old Norse literature in England and its relation to its sources', in Else Roesdahl and Preben Meulengracht Sørensen eds., *The Waking of Angantyr. The Scandinavian past in European culture, Den nordiske fortid i europæisk kultur.* Acta Jutlandica LXXI:1, Humanities Series 70. Aarhus University Press, Aarhus, Oxford and Oakville, Conn. pp. 27-57.

Fidjestøl, Bjarne 1993, 'Þorbjǫrn hornklofi', in Phillip Pulsiano and Kirsten Wolf eds., *Medieval Scandinavia. An Encyclopedia.* Garland Publishing, New York and London, pp. 668-9.

Fidjestøl, Bjarne 1997, '"Out they will look, the lovely ladies". Views of women in Norse literature', in *Selected Papers.* The Viking Collection, 9. Odense University Press, Odense, pp. 333-342.

Frank, Roberta 1990, 'Why skalds address women', in Teresa Pàroli ed., *Poetry in the Scandinavian Middle Ages. Atti del 12º Congresso Internationale di Studi sull'Alto Medioevo.* Presso la Sede del Centro di Studi, Spoleto, pp. 67-83.

Gibson, Edmund ed. 1692, *Chronicon Saxonicum ex MSS Codicibus Nunc Primum integrum Edidit, ac Latinum fecit.* Sheldonian Theatre, Oxford.

Gordon, Ian A. ed. 1952, *Shenstone's Miscellany 1759-1763.* Clarendon Press, Oxford.

G[reen], W. C. trans. 1893, *The Story of Egil Skallagrimsson: An Icelandic Family History of the Ninth and Tenth Centuries.* Elliot Stock, London.

Harris, Richard L. ed. 1992, *A Chorus of Grammars. The Correspondence of George Hickes and his Collaborators on the Thesaurus linguarum septentrionalium.* Publications of the Dictionary of Old English, 4. Pontifical Institute of Mediaeval Studies, Toronto.

Heinrichs, Anne 1993, 'Krákumál' in Phillip Pulsiano and Kirsten Wolf eds., *Medieval Scandinavia. An Encyclopedia.* Garland Publishing, New York and London, pp. 368-9.

Hickes, George *et al.* 1703-5, *Linguarum vett. septentrionalium thesaurus grammatico-criticus et archaeologicus.* 2 vols. Sheldonian Theatre,

Oxford. Facsimile reprint by Scolar Press, Menston, 1970.

Hoffmann, Marta 1964, 'The Warp-Weighted Loom. Studies in the History and Technology of an Ancient Implement'. *Studia Norvegica*, 14. Universitetsforlaget, Oslo.

Holtsmark, Anne 1939, 'Vefr Darraðar', *Maal og minne*, 74-96.

Johnstone, James 1782, *Lodbrokar-Quida; or The Death-Song of Lodbrog; now first correctly printed from various Manuscripts, with a free English translation. To which are added the various readings; a literal Latin version; an Islando-Latino glossary; and explanatory notes.* Printed for the Author, n. p.

Jónsson, Finnur ed. 1912-15, *Den norsk-islandske skjaldedigtning*. A I-II (tekst efter håndskrifterne), B I-II (rettet tekst). Gyldendal, Copenhagen, repr. Rosenkilde & Bagger, Copenhagen, 1967 (A) and 1973 (B).

Kershaw, Nora ed. and trans. 1922, *Anglo-Saxon and Norse Poems*. Cambridge University Press, Cambridge.

Lewis, Aneirin ed. 1957, *The Correspondence of Thomas Percy and Evan Evans*. The Percy Letters, V. Louisiana State University Press, n. p.

[Macpherson, James] 1760, *Fragments of Ancient Poetry, Collected in the Highlands of Scotland and Translated from the Galic or Erse Language*. G. Hamilton and J. Balfour, Edinburgh.

Mallet, Paul-Henri 1755, *Introduction à l'histoire de Dannemarc, ou l'on traite de la religion, des loix, des moeurs et des usages des anciens Danois*. n. p., Copenhagen.

Mallet, Paul-Henri 1756, *Monumens de la mythologie et de la poésie des Celtes, et particulièrement des anciens Scandinaves: pour servir de supplement et de preuves à l'introduction à l'histoire de Dannemarc*. n . p., Copenhagen.

Mallet, Paul-Henri 1763, *Introduction à l'histoire de Dannemarc, ou l'on traite de la religion, des loix, des moeurs et des usages des anciens*

Danois. 2nd. edn. 7 vols. n. p., Geneva.

Marold, Edith 1993a, 'Eyvindr Finnsson skáldaspillir', in Phillip Pulsiano and Kirsten Wolf eds., *Medieval Scandinavia. An Encyclopedia.* Garland Publishing, New York and London, pp. 175-6.

Marold, Edith 1993b, 'Einarr Helgason skálaglamm', in Phillip Pulsiano and Kirsten Wolf eds., *Medieval Scandinavia. An Encyclopedia.* Garland Publishing, New York and London, pp. 158-9.

McTurk, R. W. 1991, *Studies in Ragnars saga loðbrókar and Its Major Scandinavian Analogues.* Medium Ævum Monographs (New Series), 15. Society for the Study of Mediæval Languages and Literature, Oxford.

Nichol Smith, David ed. 1932, *Ancient Songs Chiefly on Moorish Subjects Translated from the Spanish by Thomas Percy.* Oxford University Press, Oxford.

Nordal, Sigurður ed. 1933, *Egils saga Skalla-Grímssonar.* Íslenzk Fornrit, 2. Hið íslenzka fornritafélag, Reykjavík.

Onions, C. T. ed., with the assistance of G. W. S. Friedrichsen and R. W. Burchfield 1966, *The Oxford Dictionary of English Etymology.* Oxford, Clarendon Press.

[Percy, Thomas] 1763, *Five Pieces of Runic Poetry translated from the Islandic Language.* R. and J. Dodsley, London.

[Percy, Thomas] 1765, *Reliques of Ancient English Poetry, consisting chiefly of old heroic ballads, songs, and other pieces of our earlier poets, (chiefly of the lyric kind). Together with some few of a later date.* 3 vols. J. Dodsley, London.

[Percy, Thomas] 1770, *Northern Antiquities: or, A Description of the Manners, Customs, Religion and Laws of the Ancient Danes, And other Northern Nations; Including those of Our own Saxon Ancestors. With a Translation of the Edda, or System of Runic Mythology, and other Pieces from the Ancient Islandic Tongue.* 2 vols. T. Carnan and Co., London. [2nd. edn. 1809. 3rd. edn. 1847]

Peringskiöld, Johan ed. 1697, *Heimskringla. Eller Snorre Sturlusons Nordländske Konunga Sagar Sive Historiæ Regum Septentrionalium á Snorrone Sturlonide* ....Literis Wankiwianis, Stockholm.

Poole, Russell 1985, 'Darraðarljóð 2: ǫrum hrælaðr', *Maal og minne*, 87-94.

Poole, Russell 1991, *Viking Poems on War and Peace: A study in Skaldic Narrative.* Toronto University Press, Toronto, Buffalo and London.

Poole, Russell 1993, 'Darraðarljóð', in Phillip Pulsiano and Kirsten Wolf eds., *Medieval Scandinavia. An Encyclopedia.* Garland Publishing, New York and London, p.121.

Quinn, Judy and Margaret Clunies Ross, 1994, 'The Image of Norse Poetry and Myth in Seventeenth-Century England', in Andrew Wawn ed., *Northern Antiquity. The Post-medieval Reception of Edda and Saga.* Hisarlik Press, Enfield Lock, Middlesex, pp. 189-210.

Sammes, Aylett 1676, *Britannia Antiqua Illustrata; or The Antiquities of Antient Britain.* Printed by Tho. Roycroft for the author, London.

Seaton, Ethel 1935, *Literary Relations of England and Scandinavia in the Seventeenth Century.* Clarendon Press, Oxford.

Sheringham, Robert 1670, *De Anglorum Gentis Origine Disceptatio.* Edward Story, Cambridge.

Smith, A. H. 1935, 'The Sons of Ragnar Lothbrok', *Saga-Book of the Viking Society* 11, 173-91.

Smith, Margaret M. 1998, 'Thomas Percy, William Shenstone, *Five Pieces of Runic Poetry* and the *Reliques*', *Bodleian Library Record* 12: no. 6, 471-7.

Smith, Margaret M. 1989, *Index of English Literary Manuscripts. Volume III, 1700-1800. Part 2 John Gay - Ambrose Philips*. Mansell, London and New York.

Smith, R. J. 1987, *The Gothic Bequest. Medieval Institutions in British thought, 1688-1863*. Cambridge University Press, Cambridge.

Sveinsson, Einar Ól. ed. *Brennu-Njáls saga*. Íslenzk fornrit, 12. Hið íslenzka fornritafélag, Reykjavík.

[?Thorkelín, Grímur Jónsson] *et al.* ed. and trans. 1809, *Egils-saga sive Egilli Skallagrimii vita*. Copenhagen.

Torfæus, Thormod [Þormóður Torfason] 1697, *Orcades, seu Rerum Orcadensium historiæ libri tres*. Literis Justini Hög, Universit. Typogr., Havniæ [Copenhagen].

Turville-Petre, Gabriel 1968, *Harald the Hard-ruler and his Poets*. The Dorothea Coke Memorial Lecture in Northern Studies, 1966. University College London.

Verelius, Olaus ed. 1672, *Hervarar Saga på Gammal Götska*. Excudit Henricus Curio S. R. M. & Academiæ Upsaliensis Bibliopola, Uppsala.

Warton, Thomas 1774, *The History of English Poetry, from the Close of the Eleventh to the Commencement of the Eighteenth Century*. Vol.1 [vols. 2 and 3 were published in 1778 and 1781 respectively] J. Dodsley, London and Messrs. Fletcher, Oxford.

Wawn, Andrew 2000, *The Vikings and the Victorians. Inventing the Old North in Nineteenth-Century Britain*. D. S. Brewer, Cambridge.

Whaley, Diana Edwards 1993a, 'Skalds and situational verses in *Heimskringla*', in Alois Wolf ed., *Snorri Sturluson. Kolloquium anläßlich der 750. Wiederkehr seines Todestages*. Gunter Narr Verlag, Tübingen, pp. 245-266.

Whaley, Diana Edwards 1993b 'Heimskringla', in Phillip Pulsiano and Kirsten Wolf eds., *Medieval Scandinavia. An Encyclopedia*. Garland Publishing, New York and London, pp. 276-279.

Wilson, David and Ole Klindt-Jensen 1966, *Viking Art*. Allen & Unwin, London.

Worm, Ole 1636, *RUNER, seu Danica Literatura Antiqvissima, Vulgo Gothica dicta, luci reddita. opera O. Wormii; acc. de prisca Danorum poesi dissertatio* [referred to as *Literatura Runica*]. Apud Joannem Jansonium, Amsterdam.

Index

Note: Traditional Icelandic names are listed alphabetically by given name followed by patronymic, e.g. Árni Magnússon. All other names are listed alphabetically by surname.